If Not Higher

If Not Higher

Stories and Insights of
Rabbi Yehuda Kelemer zt"l

by
Dr. Stuart Apfel
Hanoch Teller

New York Publishing Company
A division of M.E.T. llc

Rechov Yehoyariv 4/7, Arzei Habira, Jerusalem 9735418, Israel
www.hanochteller.com
Cover picture: Ari Hirsch

10 8 6 4 2
9 7 5 3 1

Library of Congress Control Number: 2023949188

ISBN 978-1-881939-28-3

Distributed by:

FELDHEIM PUBLISHERS
www.feldheim.com

J. LEHMANN
Hebrew Booksellers
www.lehmanns.co.uk/home.html

KULMUS
0722-44-166

Podcast:

TellerFromJerusalem.com

Dedicated in honor
of the esteemed members of
the קהילות הקודש of Brookline, Massachusetts
and West Hempstead, New York.

You continuously sought the guidance of your
Mara D'asra, Rav Yehuda Kelemer,
striving to elevate your lives by following his
stellar example of Torah and *chesed*.

Your insatiable thirst for growth
gave him much *nachas* and inspiration
to continue his עבודת הקודש.

May we merit to uphold his memory
and his Torah teachings.

וְכָל בָּנַיִךְ לִמּוּדֵי ה' וְרַב שְׁלוֹם בָּנָיִךְ

ROCHEL KELEMER AND FAMILY

Lovingly Dedicated by
the West Hempstead Community
in Memory of our *Mara D'asra*

HaRav Yehuda Kelemer *zt"l*

For nearly four decades we were blessed with
a תלמיד חכם, פוסק, בעל חסד, צדיק ומלאך
in our midst to guide, teach and comfort us.
His pure mind and golden heart felt the pain
of every Jew and celebrated their every joy.

החותמים בדמע:

Stuart and Beth Alter
Jonathan and Sari Altmark
Stuart and Sari Apfel
David and Tzippora Baratz
Larry and Sharona Beck
Menachem and Leah Brick
Bruce and Adina Broder
Simeon and Beth Chiger
Arthur and Jani Cooperberg
Beryl and Doreen Eckstein
Shimmie and Karen Ehrenreich
Alan and Judi Eisenman
Richard and Sheri Feldman
Dovid and Adina Frankel
Gary and Michele Friedman
Nechemia and Chanie Ginsburg
Alan and Cookie Greene
Ari and Alison Gross
Richard and Anita Grossman
Robert and Melody Harris
Ari and Rina Hirsch
Yitzy and Naomi Hollander
Yossi and Adina Hollander
Zev and Rifky Isseroff
Marc and Sharon Katz
Dov and Amy Kesselman
David Ari and Reva Kirshblum
Tsvi and Ruchi Kushner
Stephen and Naomi Lassar
Arnold and Millie Levine
Joshua and Kari Levine
Michael and Simcha Levine
Harvey Liebman
Seymour and Mindy Liebman
William and Sharon Lovy
Aaron and Shani Malitzky
Bob and Gila Margulies
Samuel and Miriam Meyer
Richard and Reva Miller
Moshe and Cali Orenbuch
Abe and Sara Peller
Nejat and Hilda Rahmani
Penny Kraut and Paul Reinstein
David and Robin Ritholtz
Martin and Helen Schiowitz
Avi and Rochelle Schneider
Tzvi and Erica Schwartz
Steven and Dina Selesney
Alan and Sharon Shulman
Morris and Devorah Smith
Marc and Esther Soskel
Jeremy and Meryl Strauss
Howard and Nechama Taber
Mark S. Cohen
and Roberta Weinstein
Yossi and Sharon Wiesel
David and Ivy Yizhaky
Izzy Zehnwirth
Lenny and Amy Zehnwirth
Shaun and Michelle Zeitlin

Also by
Hanoch Teller

Once Upon a Soul
Soul Survivors
'Souled!'
The Steipler Gaon
Sunset
Courtrooms of the Mind
Above the Bottom Line
Pichifkes
The Bostoner
"Hey, Taxi!"
Bridges of Steel, Ladders of Gold
The Best of StoryLines
Give Peace a Stance
It's a Matter of Principal
A Midrash and a Maaseh
Welcome to the Real World
13 Years
And from Jerusalem, HIS Word
It's a Small Word, After All
The MINI A Midrash and a Maaseh
In an Unrelated Story...
Builders
Too Beautiful
For the Love of Torah
Heroic Children
О Том, Что На Душе
Героизм Нашей Души
ועמך כולם...
בצדק תשפט
Érase Una Vez
Desde Jerusalem...

The Righteous Live On (Audio Series)
Comprehending the Incomprehensible (Audio Series)
Building Bene Brak (Audio Series)
Do You Believe in Miracles (Video Documentary)
Reb Elimelech and the Chassidic Legacy of Brotherhood
(Video Documentary)
We're All in This Together (Video Satire)

"Teller From Jerusalem" Podcast

APPROBATION OF
HARAV SHMUEL KAMENETSKY Shlita

שמואל קמנצקי
Rabbi S. Kamenetsky

2018 Upland Way
Philadelphia, PA 19131

Home: 215-473-2798
Study: 215-473-1212

בס"ד

ג' חשון, תשפ"ד

למע"כ הרב ר' חנוך טלר שליט"א,

שמעתי שאתה עומד להוציא לאור ספר אודות חייו ופעולותיו של מחותני היקר והבלתי נשכח הרה"ג ר' יהודה קלמר זצ"ל. ידוע, שמלבד גאונותו בתורה בנגלה ובנסתר, הי' משפיע כסדר על אלפי מאחינו בית ישראל ומשפחותיהן. כמעט שאין איש או אשה שבא במגע אתו שלא יצא עם דבר חכמה או סתם חיזוק שהאציל מאישיותו החמה והלבבית.

ברכתי שהספר יהי' לתועלת גדולה לכל הקוראים בו, ושיזכה בכ' להוציא עוד ספרים אחרים ויהנו מהם רבים.

APPROBATION OF
HARAV ZEV LEFF Shlita

בס"ד

Rabbi Zev Leff — הרב זאב לף

Rabbi of Moshav Matityahu — מרא דאתרא מושב מתתיהו

Rosh HaYeshiva—Yeshiva Gedola Matityahu — ראש הישיבה—ישיבה גדולה מתתיהו

D.N. Modiin 71917 | Tel: 08-976-1138 טל' | Fax: 08-976-5326 פקס' | ד.נ. מודיעין 71917

ב מרחשון תשפ"ד
October, 17, 2023

Dear Friends,

I have read portions of the book "If Not Higher" by Rabbi Hanoch Teller. The book is a biography of Rabbi Yehuda Kelemer ZT"L. Although, I usually do not give haskamos to the genre of novels or biographies, I feel compelled to offer my bracha and praise for this book in particular. My path and the path of Rabbi Kelemer have almost crossed numerous times. We both grew up in Miami, and attended the Hebrew Academy, albeit not at the same time. Rabbi Dr. Max Lipshitz who was a great support to my parents and to myself in my childhood years many times boasted of his nephews "Jordy" and Yisroel Kelemer. When I came to learn in Telshe Yeshiva, Yehuda Kelemer had already left to Eretz Yisroel, but his name was a legend in the Yeshiva as a true illuy (genius) whom my Rebbe, HaRav Mordechai Gifter ZT"L chose as a chavrusa and with whom he learned yevamos numerous times. We both became Young Israel Rabbis and I had the merit to consult with him and interact with him on a few occasions. Although reading this book made me feel inadequate as a Rabbi, dwarfed by this Rabbinic giant, I am proud to have had even a fleeting connection with such a Torah giant.

Additionally, my esteemed friend and colleague, Rabbi Hanoch Teller has revealed and expressed the greatness of Rabbi Kelemer in his so many facets in such a masterful and magnificent manner, as only a Talmid Chochom, educator, and literary professional that he is, could possibly accomplish.

I, therefore, commend Rabbi Teller for producing another masterpiece that will inspire and enlighten the community with the biography of such a literal angelic personality.

I pray that Hashem bless Rabbi Teller and his family with life, health and the wherewithal to continue to merit the community in his many and varied ways.

Sincerely,
With Torah blessings

Zev Leff

Rabbi Zev Leff

APPROBATION OF HARAV YITZCHAK BREITOWITZ Shlita

מוסדות אור שמח מרכז טננבאום ע.ר. 58-00-21343-00
רח' שמעון הצדיק 22-28 ירושלים ת.ד. 18103
טל: 02-581-0315

Michtav Bracha

Cheshvan 5784

Rabbi Yehudah Kelemer z"l was an outstanding rav in every respect -a phenomenal talmid chacham ,a tremendous masmid who learned every minute he could ,an expert posek ,a kind compassionate heart willing to give unlimited time to any Jew in need.He was a person who greeted **everyone** b'sever panim yafos .Inspite of his brilliance ,he was a modest humble man who encouraged and built up other rabbonim and mosdos giving them the confidence to do their jobs .I was zoche to know him when he was still a relatively-young rav in Brookline ,Massachusets (when I was a freshman law student) and even then ,his greatness was apparent .With the passage of time ,his gadlus would become more and more evident .Despite his humble ,relatively-low profile ,his petira was an enormous loss not only for West Hempstead but for all of Klal Yisrael.

My dear friend Reb Hanoch Teller has written a wonderful book which vividly captures the many facets of Rabbi Kelemer's personality - the moach and the lev ,the brilliant mind and the compassionate feeling heart .This is not just a book of interesting stories though it surely is that - but a book of mussar calling on all of us to be bigger ,greater ,better;to aspire to go beyond our comfort zone ;to combine fidelity to halacha with ethical sensitivity ; to make the name of Hashem and His Torah beloved in the eyes of others .In that way ,Rabbi Kelemer will continue to teach us even after his death the great lessons he taught us in his life .Yehi zichro baruch !

With Admiration and Bracha,

Yitzchak A. Breitowitz
Rav ,Kehillas Ohr Somayach

APPROBATION OF HARAV ARYEH LEBOWITZ Shlita

Rabbi Aryeh Lebowitz

ה' חשון תשפ"ד

We often have a tendency to only appreciate greatness after it is taken from us. A great person passes away, and suddenly people notice their greatness through their absence. Other times, a world famous gadol or tzadik walks among us and everybody is aware during his lifetime how privileged we are to have this gift. Rav Yehuda Kelemer זצ"ל fits into a third category. On the one hand, Rav Kelemer's greatness was not known throughout the world. He operated in a little corner of the world called West Hempstead, and he devoted all of his energies to his beloved community. On the other hand, every single person who interacted with Rav Kelemer זצ"ל and lived within his orbit, readily understood that they were in the presence of greatness. You can stop any member of the West Hempstead community and ask what their "Rav Kelemer story" is, and they will immediately produce a story that sounds as if it was said about a tzadik who lived hundreds of years earlier. Anybody who knew Rav Kelemer only wondered who the *other* 35 hidden tzadikim of our generation are.

In today's world, there are many people who communicate with, and inspire, thousands of people at a time. They accomplish this through the medium of modern technology and other methods. Rav Kelemer also affected thousands of people in life changing ways, but he did so by impacting one person at a time.

I was so gratified to learn that Rav Hanoch Teller, a dear friend and somebody who I admire greatly, took on the holy task and responsibility of bringing Rav Kelemer's story to the broader Jewish world. In a time where that which Rav Kelemer זצ"ל stood for is so desperately needed, it takes a person of unique spiritual sensitivity, a person who antennae are up and able to comprehend the nuances of greatness in each act, to fully present the inspirational life of Rav Kelemer to the world.

I would warn the reader that one can be at once inspired and dejected when reading about Rav Kelemer. Please understand that none of us are expected to be quite like Rav Kelemer. He was a giant. The last thing he would want is for anybody to feel small after reading this book. He excelled at making everybody feel so big, so honorable, and so worthy. As we read about greatness we should be filled with a sense of gratitude that we were able to interact with such a person, and inspiration to enhance our own love of Hashem and His children in some small way.

Aryeh Lebowitz

649 Hungry Harbor Road • North Woodmere NY 11581 • 516-295-1491
www.bknw.org

Contents

Approbations . . . . *IX*
Acknowledgments . . . . *XV*
Preface . . . . *XXI*
Author's Note . . . . *XXVII*
Introduction . . . . *XXXI*

ONE / Every Symphony Needs a Conductor . . *33*

TWO / The Life of Rabbi Yehuda Kelemer *49*

THREE / The Magic of Making a *Psak* Work . . *63*

FOUR / Every Student Was Important *89*

FIVE / More Than a Phone Call *103*

SIX / Under the *Chuppah* *117*

SEVEN / Like a *Sefer Torah* *133*

EIGHT / I Will Be Right There *147*

NINE / His Busiest and Most Stressful Day . . *189*

TEN / One Who Walks with Kings *213*

ELEVEN / Too Multifaceted *229*

TWELVE / I Have Failed as a Rav,
If Such a Question Could Be Asked . . . *241*

GLOSSARY *272*

Acknowledgments

Completing a book is always a merciless battle against a deadline. If we prefer (as the Talmud encourages) to employ refined language, this could be referred to as a "due date."[1] Factually, Rabbi Yehuda Kelemer came up with his own term regarding a different matter, for perhaps the very same reason. He would say that his phone battery had "discharged," as opposed to the more conventional "died."

For me, the upside of completion is the privilege to write acknowledgements. If there is anything that I share in common with Rabbi Kelemer *zt"l*, it is that we were both privileged to learn under and be influenced by the paramount Mirrer

---

1. Gratitude to my friend Rabbi Joseph Telushkin, who saw the wisdom of replacing a term that has a negative connotation with a term that has such a positive association.

Rosh Yeshivah, Rav Chaim Shmuelevitz *zt"l*. Rav Chaim was most famous for his discourses on gratitude. Whoever was privileged to hear them has an edge in this regard.

Firstly, thanks to Rebbetzin Kelemer, who ensured that the book would be a faithful reflection of the life and the ideals of the subject. It was such a delightful surprise for me to learn that the Rebbetzin is the sister of the man I looked up to so much, my dear friend, Rav Chaim Walkin *zt"l*. I should mention that of course she is also sister-in-law to Rebbetzin Henny Walkin, co-founder of the *Jewish Women's Outlook*, which had such a profound effect upon my writing career.

My esteemed co-author I acknowledge separately in the Author's Note.

Mrs. Karen Smith worked expeditiously to speed the book along. Rabbi Josh Goller from the Young Israel of West Hempstead was always available for me, and it was supportive to know that if a question would arise I could always turn to him and he would respond as quickly as possible.

There are three women that were of pivotal assistance to me in this project. They are: Mrs. Dvora Freimark was kind (and forceful) enough to exert editorial privilege to ensure the book's timely publication.

Hannah Hartman consistently and perpetually offers me the greatest typesetting, no matter what the time crunch. If other people that I collaborate with had her work ethic, I would be so much more productive.

And leaving the best for last, Professor Vera Schwarcz graciously and magnanimously jumped in during her vacation time and figured out (there is nothing that she cannot figure out) how to graft two disparate authors into one cohesive book.

When I must conclude a project, it requires total immersion and I thank my wife Aidel for being so *aidel* to enable me to disappear — either physically or, for all intents and purposes, metaphorically.

David Schulman understood the urgency of rushing the book's manufacture and did not penalize in the cost (so welcome in a time that Chapter 11 has become as familiar as Catch-22). Kudos to Mrs. Yonina Lederer, who assists me with reliability and competence.

Eli Meir Hollander and the Feldheim Publishing House are the greatest, most honest, friendliest and most considerate people to work with in this galaxy. Decades and dozens of books are all a testament to this of such certitude that you can bet the house on it and throw in the mortgage.

Here is an opportunity to acknowledge two dear friends that are both the persons that I would want to be if I did not have to be myself. I am forever grateful to Refael Leib Rosenberg and Rav Gil Frieman for letting this nerdlet join their bond and permitting me a boarding pass to nobility. Speaking of friendship, our children and their spouses authenticate the aphorism, "blood is thicker..."

How apt it is to acknowledge in my Acknowledgments the dynamic duo in Kansas City with whom I learn with every week. Dr. Howard Rosenthal and Matt Siegel manage to teach me so much in just one weekly installment. No one knows better than I what makes Kansas City royal.

Ditto to Dr. Diane Medved. How lucky can I be? She can crack in an instant conundrums that have mystified the godfathers of wholesale wisdom for hundreds of years.

The Talmud (*Eiruvin* 54b) says that Rav Preida would teach a disciple 400(!) times until it sank in. Asked Rav Chaim Shmuelevitz, how could Rav Preida allow for such a hemorrhage of his time? He answered that for Rav Preida this was not a learning session, but rather a *mussar seder*. I think of this often in context of Rabbi Shimon Bertman, Rabbi Aaron David and Rabbi Yitzchak Grant learning with me.

Lastly, I humbly thank the Almighty for enabling me to bring yet another book to press. The book came out of nowhere and I resisted getting involved for well over a year until I was, and remain, several facts short of a clue as to why my involvement was meant to be.

Preface

The story goes,[2] according to Yiddish writer I.L. Peretz, that a Lithuanian *misnaged* (opposer of the chassidic movement) chanced upon a chassidic town during the Ten Days of Repentance between Rosh Hashanah and Yom Kippur. During these days, it is customary to rise early and recite *Selichos* (the penitential prayers) in the synagogue.

To the amazement of the *misnaged* guest, the Rebbe was not present for *Selichos*. The *chassidim* explained the Rebbe's absence with the outrageous assertion that he had ascended to heaven to recite *Selichos*! Maybe it was the mention of "heaven" that caused the *misnaged* to look at the *chassidim* as if they had

2. I have never read it in Yiddish or any other language, so I am taking some liberties with my rendering.

just arrived on a flying saucer from some outer galactic super cluster. Meanwhile, the *chassidim* began to swoon at the very mention of their Rebbe. Some of them closed their eyes in bliss, while others thrust their arms into the air in case the *misnaged* was unfamiliar with the location of heaven.

"Huh?!" the *misnaged* regurgitated, his eyebrows jump-roping in incredulity. But the *chassidim* continued to nod their heads in agreement as if they had just stated an absolutely irrefutable fact.

"You don't really believe this?" the *misnaged* questioned — apparently to no one, for his disputants had beamed up to nirvana at the mere mention of their Rebbe. The *misnaged* saw that there was no one with which to conduct a sane conversation; he felt as useless as a dentist in a town where everyone had false teeth.

Maybe, he thought in desperation, if the Rebbe would deign to come to *Selichos* the next day, he could confront the grand Rabbi as to where he had been. Despite being ensconced in a sheltered shoal of unworldly innocents, surely the Rebbe would not be so brazen and shameless to claim that he had been up in heaven reciting *Selichos*! It was similarly unlikely that the Rebbe would admit that he had overslept, but the *misnaged* felt he would be capable of seeing through any excuse.

But the next day the Rebbe also wasn't there. The early penitential prayers continued with everyone beating their chests in remorse over their past misdeeds, as the Rebbe surely continued to turn over in his sleep! Just to be certain — in the unlikely event the *chassidim* had been stirred from their reverie — the *misnaged* inquired again as to where the Rebbe was, and received precisely the same answer.

Wait until he'd return home and would tell his fellow *misnagdim* about what he had experienced. The few who were still soft-hearted about *chassidim* would surely change their attitude after his report from Toontown.

Then the *misnaged* had yet a different idea. He would get up very early the next day and lie in ambush outside the Rebbe's house. This way, he would be able to report exactly where the Rebbe was while everyone else was where they were supposed to be — reciting *Selichos* in shul.

In the early hours of the next morning, the *misnaged*, deeply camouflaged, lay in wait across from the Rebbe's house. His eyes trained on the Rebbe's door, he did not expect it to open for a good few hours. It was worth missing *Selichos*, he felt, to puncture the bubble of these hopelessly gullible *chassidim*.

The *misnaged* did not have to wait long. In the early pre-dawn hours, the Rebbe stepped out of his door with an axe over his shoulder and a looped bundle of cordage at his hip. The air was zesty, and a blue-edged circle formed an angelic corona around the waning crescent moon. Spears of frozen breath issued forth from the Rebbe's mouth, and at least they were heading heavenward. The Rebbe set a brisk pace as he headed out into the woods, and the *misnaged*, at a safe distance, followed every step. Suddenly the Rebbe stopped and carefully examined the tree in front of him, as if he had found what he was after. The *misnaged* had not banked on this adventure and was unable to process all that he was beholding.

The Rebbe placed the rope on the ground. And then, as if he were an experienced lumberjack, he took aim and swung at the trunk, creating a notch. With repeated blows between the knee and the waist, he persisted to strike until the tree was felled. The Rebbe then made quick work of chopping the tree into manageable logs, tied them all together and hoisted them onto his shoulder. In great haste — as if he had several other tasks to complete before dawn — the Rebbe headed out of the woods in a different direction than he had entered.

The mystified *misnaged* attempted to keep pace until the Rebbe reached a path. The Grand Rabbi turned his head in both directions to assure himself that the coast was clear and his movements were not being detected. He then raced over to a widow's hovel, deposited the firewood anonymously at her doorstep and vanished.

There wasn't much illumination, the night just barely alight from the twinkling stars, but what the misnaged had just witnessed was incontrovertible. Remorse gnawing at his conscience, the *misnaged* made his way to shul for *Selichos*. When he completed his prayers, a *chassid* approached him and asked matter-of-factly, "What do you say about our Rebbe who recites *Selichos* in heaven?"

All the *misnaged* could reply was, "*Oib nisht noch hecher* — If not higher!"

Other than Sholem Aleichem's tales of Tevye the milkman (popularized in *Fiddler on the Roof*), most people are not familiar with the stories of 19th century Yiddish writers — with the exception of the members of the Young Israel of West Hempstead. Many of the congregants have heard of Peretz's tale "If Not Higher" as a reference to describe the indescribable Rabbi Yehuda Kelemer. Whatever you say about him, it displays (as he would have preferred) serious incomprehension of the complete picture. The wondrous accounts of Rabbi Kelemer's kindness, magnanimity, scholarship, humility, halachic expertise and more, fail to fully describe who the man was and what he accomplished. Whatever someone said about him, the only judicious response was, "If not higher!"

And yet, even the legend of the Rebbe and the *misnaged*, used for purely parabolic purposes, fails in two ways to do justice to Rabbi Kelemer. The point of the story is the championing of kindness, anonymous charity and concern for the less fortunate over religious rites. Peretz was, after all, a secular humanist.

For Rabbi Kelemer there was never a challenge, conflict or need to prioritize between his *mentschlichkeit* and his *Yiddishkeit*. They were not just symbiotic, and parts of the same; they were one and the same. Rabbi Kelemer the angel of benevolence could never be separated from Rabbi Kelemer the *Gadol baTorah*. His every action broadcast how immersion in Torah study is supposed to influence one's actions.

The second dissimilarity is that Rabbi Kelemer had no skeptics. Everyone was in awe of his character and would never challenge his wisdom.

Author's Note

THIS SECTION HAS BEEN subtitled "Author's Note" in compliance with conventional metawriting. Factually, there are *two* authors to this book: the esteemed Dr. Stuart Apfel and yours truly. Dr. Apfel and I did not work jointly, conjunctionally or symbiotically. Dr. Apfel meticulously collected the reminisces of the community and codified them into thematic chapters. After his work was completed, I entered with an attempt to round out certain aspects that deserved a tad more attention.

The reader will have no confusion discerning what was rendered by Dr. Apfel and what I have written (independent of the fact that whatever Stu wrote or collected is in italics, and mine is in Roman). Our prose couldn't be more different. Dr. Apfel is a brilliant physician accustomed to writing scientific papers, and my style is florid and descriptive. Anecdotes submitted by community members were left in their authentic voice and pronunciation (even at the expense of the book's uniformity).

Non-stylistically, it must be pointed out that Rabbi Kelemer did not have a monopoly on outstanding, noble character; it permeates the entire

Kelemer household. Ironically, this presented a thorny difficulty for this writer regarding insights and stories about the life of Rabbi Kelemer, *zt"l*.

One could hear a fantastic and wonderfully reflective story about Rabbi Kelemer, write it down and submit it to the family, only for them to become uneasy. "Oish! Mr. Shwartz will think this is referring to him as the last name rhymes with his daughter-in-law's maiden name." "How could we ever publish this, for Mrs. Greenbaum will think we are referring to the time she went to her neighbors for a meal on Shabbos and they weren't expecting her?" "Could you imagine? If we write this anecdote about Dov then Leon will be upset that we didn't write something about him as well."

I hope the reader is getting my drift that these were not the ideal circumstances for an author to operate. I was not plagued or panged by these dilemmas. In dealing with the Kelemer family, it seemed there was almost *too much* consideration, sensitivity, respect and *middos*. It was a constant challenge.

So here is where my drawback became an asset. I never lived in West Hempstead and visited very infrequently. Accordingly, I was deprived of the exposure to Rabbi Kelemer that surely would have enriched my life, as it did for everyone else he encountered. On the other hand, precisely because I am outsider, I need not worry that my words will prove offensive, for everyone understands that (even if I was told a story in the name of the protagonist) I do not know who I was writing about.

This was a hard stance to take with the Kelemers, for they were always worried about the slightest possible infringement regarding the feelings of others. Ultimately, I had to assert a little author prerogative, for even if I could tolerate walking on eggshells (I can't) I had to put my foot down (unfortunate expression in this instance) to the perception and fear of walking on eggshells in spiked track shoes.

Therefore, in the unlikely event that there may be a line to which an individual may take offense for fear that it does not reflect upon them in the most charitable light, trust me, I was not writing about you! Even if a similar incident happened to *you*, the chances that I knew about it are infinitesimal. Thank you for your consideration.

Hanoch (Outsider) Teller
עש"ק פרשת נח תשפ"ד ירושלים ת"ו
October 20, 2023
היום ה–14 לחרבות ברזל

Introduction:

How in the World Did Rabbi Kelemer Slip In?

One wondrous moment in October 2015 captures the unique personality and mission of the singular Rabbi Yehuda Kelemer. It happened in the presence of Nesanel Feller, who was not a member of the Rabbi's shul in West Hempstead. Though Mr. Feller himself did not reside in the town, his in-laws and relatives did, and he received the same attention and devotion that Rabbi Kelemer afforded everyone he knew, congregant or not.

A decade ago, it was not commonplace for people to donate kidneys. Nesanel was an exception, and his altruism caught Rabbi Kelemer's attention. The most unusual part of the story — unless you knew Rabbi Kelemer — was the identity of Nesanel's first post-surgery visitor.

Still in the recovery room, Nesanel was anesthetized and groggy, and certainly not in a position to see who was coming and going. It was still beyond Sherlock Feller's ability to even open his eyes.

But he was awake enough to hear the buzz of medical personnel, the whoosh of machines and the thump of monitors. And then, in the midst of all of this hospital ambience, he heard the friendly voice of Rabbi Kelemer extending greetings and blessings. This was something to wake up to!

The Rabbi was the first one to greet him in a room that was sterile, other than the gowned surgical staff — way ahead of Nesanel's family, who were waiting anxiously outside.

But with Nesanel Feller's immediate family gathered outside the recovery room in Manhattan's ultra parking-non-friendly and super-by-the-book Columbia Presbyterian Hospital, how in the world did Rabbi Kelemer slip in?

This question arose again and again during the decades of unassuming and astounding leadership provided by Rabbi Yehuda Kelemer wherever he went. The deepest legacy left by this remarkable scholar and mentor remains in the Young Israel of West Hempstead community, which he guided from 1983 until his untimely death on January 8, 2021.

CHAPTER ONE

Every Symphony Needs a Conductor

With a membership of 750 families, the Young Israel of West Hempstead is a hive of activity every day of the week. The peak, of course, is Shabbos, with multiple *minyanim*, activities and *shiurim* taking place simultaneously. Every symphony needs a conductor, and Rabbi Kelemer figuratively held his baton aloft from *Kabbalas Shabbos* through *Havdalah*.

Beyond his "conductor" role, Rabbi Kelemer needed to be both manager and soul physician in order to triage and assess what needed acute attention and what could be postponed. In this regard, Rabbi Kelemer "failed." He afforded his attention to everything, and nothing was insignificant in his eyes.

The Young Israel of West Hempstead is an Orthodox shul located on Long Island — the second largest Young Israel in the United States. The shul blossomed, as it was blessed with an extraordinary Rabbi who appeared to transcend the mundane world in which his congregants lived. He was able to rise to celestial heights while remaining very much down to earth and eminently relatable. A big *machlokes* (controversy) in the community focused on whether the Rabbi could best be characterized as a *tzaddik* (a completely righteous individual), a *Gadol baTorah* (eminent, world class Torah scholar), or a *malach* (divine angel). Most held that all three applied. While the last characterization might appear an exaggeration, for those who witnessed Rabbi Kelemer's actions far beyond the natural world, there was no other explanation for how he often appeared to be in two places at once, how he managed on so little sleep, or how he weathered the weight of the many sufferings that he carried constantly in his mind.

On Erev Shabbos, January 8, 2021, the West Hempstead community, along with thousands of other Jews throughout the world, suffered a painful, traumatic loss, when Rabbi Yehuda Kelemer passed away at the age of 74. For most, the loss was as painful as the passing of a close relative, perhaps even a father. In truth, he was like a father to his congregants and to members of the larger West Hempstead community, as well as to his previous *kehillah* (congregation) in Boston. Tragically, the world lost not only his brilliant mind and encyclopedic knowledge of Torah, which were legendary. More importantly, the nation lost his immeasurable acts of *chesed* and his near superhuman efforts to care for every human being in need.

No issue was ever too small or beyond his purview. He lived to be of service to others. Each person Rabbi Kelemer knew was left feeling that the Rabbi had no concern other than to help that individual at that moment. Rabbi Kelemer never waited for someone to approach him with a problem. He actively sought out and approached those who possibly needed his help.

One Shabbos morning, as Rabbi Kelemer was speed-walking down the hall of the Young Israel from one event to the next, he saw a little girl, no older than four years old, crying. Luckily, Rabbi Kelemer was equipped for emergencies like these, and handed the little girl a lollipop. Apparently, it was just what the doctor ordered, for her rather shrill pipes fell silent. The problem was solved and the Rabbi was on his way to solve the next crisis.

But just a few moments later, returning in the opposite direction, he found the little girl just where he had left her, lollipop in hand, poised to begin her gastronomic adventure. Rabbi Kelemer lowered himself to the ground next to her and offered, "Let us make a *brachah* (blessing) together, with all of our heart!"

Every Shabbos and Yom Tov night, following *Maariv* services, he would walk all around West Hempstead visiting the elderly, the sick, or those who might require help or companionship. His family knew never to expect him to come home until late at night. Even after his serious accident, he continued this sacred task of visiting all who might need him, albeit with a walker. Through example, he taught his community to act with the same generous *middos* — character traits that mark a truly Torah-loving Jew.

He was an outstanding speaker and teacher who could easily mesmerize the audience with his soft voice that expressed profoundly powerful ideas, yet his most important lessons were silent ones. He demonstrated how to behave as an *eved HaShem* (a servant of the Almighty) every waking moment.

Say Little, Do a Lot

AT HIS INSTALLATION as Rabbi of the Young Israel of West Hempstead, Rabbi Kelemer expressed his hope to fulfill the teaching of Shamai from *Pirkei Avos: emor me'at va'aseh harbeh* — say little, but do a great deal (1:14). While he was eminently successful, none of Rabbi Kelemer's numerous accomplishments would have been possible without the constant help and support of his *eishes chayil* Rochi. Rebbetzin Kelemer was often by the Rabbi's side as he performed his numerous acts of *chesed*. She raised their large family, many a time while her husband was attending to his Rabbinic duties — as she enabled and encouraged him to care for everyone in need.

Rabbi Kelemer knew the birthdays of each child in his *kehillah* and made sure that the child's parents were able to provide a gift to mark the occasion. Without any fanfare, he collaborated with a congregant in organizing Chanukah drives with gift cards that needy families could use to purchase presents for their children. If there was money left from what was earmarked for Chanukah gifts, he would propose that the families use it for birthday presents.

Rabbi Kelemer knew a lot more than just the children's birthdays. He was aware of the personal problems of the younger members of his congregation, and he had an uncanny sense for detecting an issue. Often, he would suggest that he take them out to eat to discuss what was troubling them, and to work out a path forward.

Rabbi Kelemer understood that getting through to the kids entailed more than just grabbing them at the right age. It also meant conversing with them where they were comfortable, and that was not necessarily the Rabbi's office.

One of Rabbi Kelemer's favorite go-tos was the local kosher Chinese restaurant, Wing Wan. Rabbi Kelemer was the *Rav hamachshir* and he arranged to come with his young charge at closing hours as the restaurant was closing down. This afforded them some privacy in a public setting (along with dumplings in Szechuan sauce).

After every meeting when it became time to pay, Amy, the proprietress and daughter-in-law of the original owner, became elusive — but there was no way that the Rabbi was going to eat or treat, and then not pay for it. He would always track her down and ask, "How much do I owe?"

And the proprietress would respond, *every single time*, "Rabbi, don't worry about it."

But clearly the Rabbi *was* worried, concerned and anxious about benefitting without remunerating. "I must pay," the Rabbi declared in a low, disappointed-in-humanity tone as his voice fell an octave.

Amy put up a valiant fight, but always capitulated (at least symbolically) in the end. "Okay, Rabbi, five dollars." Often, Amy would send the Rabbi home with extra food, which Rabbi Kelemer always knew how to distribute to the needy.

And now, the back story: Wing Wan was an established Chinese restaurant, serving the general non-kosher public of West Hempstead.

Wing Wan's operating expenses were not much different than those of any other restaurant, but its revenue streams were limited, with a dearth of beverage sales, merchandise, gift cards, packaged goods, and the like.

Mr. Wong, the owner, observing the exponential growth of the religious Jewish community, approached Rabbi Kelemer and asked if he could assist in turning his restaurant into a kosher establishment. The Rabbi response was, in many ways, similar to the reply to someone who wishes to convert to Judaism. "A kosher restaurant will entail an awful amount of work. It will be very laborious to make it kosher, and then will require a lot of effort and expense to keep it kosher."[3]

Mr. Wong responded simply, "No pain, no gain." He understood that if he wished to tap into an exploding market he was going to have to work hard — and he already knew the alternative. Working hard was a legitimate price for the likelihood of quadrupling sales — indeed, a no-brainer.

For all of the Rabbi's work and significant hours in kashering the kitchen, he took not a penny. Nor did he charge for offering his *hashgachah*. Some readers may be familiar with the

3. The Rabbi knew of what he spoke. When he was a Rabbi in Brookline he kashered the Queensbury Bakery, which had originated, or certainly seized the wave, of whole wheat *challos*, which had not been heard of before.

costs usually involved in such an enterprise and appreciate the Rabbi's largesse. What was in it for the Rabbi was the need for the community the size of the Young Israel to have a kosher restaurant.

Despite the fortune that Rabbi Kelemer had brought to Amy's coffers, he would never countenance a free meal. And thus, they invariably repeated the same exchange, as can be attested by so many boys from West Hempstead.

As the Rabbi felt that he had landed a successful venue for the youth at Wing Wan, he also organized for a Rabbi from Far Rockaway to deliver a weekly *shiur* to the youth from West Hempstead on whom he wanted to keep an eye. All the young men had to do was show up for a weekly free meal, and dessert was served with a *dvar Torah*. It was win-win all around at Wing Wan.

As far as the Rabbi was concerned, his restaurant expenses were a small price to monitor the boys at an often-challenging age. For the participants, a short *dvar Torah* was a small price for Beef Yat Gum Mein.

Rabbi Kelemer confessed to a congregant that going out to eat proved to be an effective strategy for only half the teens in town. He was uncomfortable going out to eat with females, and needed to devise a strategy that would be effective for the distaff side. Rabbi Kelemer was never at ease if he felt that he was not doing all that he could to help.

This very congregant related that as he was driving home one Tuesday close to midnight, he saw two men on the street, one of them wearing a black hat. He slowed down to offer a ride, and then discovered that it was Rabbi Kelemer talking to a young man. So as not to cause embarrassment he hit the gas pedal, careful not to notice who was getting some of the Rabbi's personal attention.

One day, the occasion presented itself for this fellow to question Rabbi Kelemer about that late-night oddity. The Rabbi replied matter-of-factly that there was a youth with autism who was most approachable late at night. The Rabbi would therefore take walks with this young man at that hour, to extend companionship to an individual who did not have a plethora of friends.

As one of the Rabbi's sons, Shmuel Dovid, pointed out at his *levayah*, "Every encounter he had with anyone was another story in itself, as he uplifted and made people feel special in a way they may never have before." Community members often tell stories that illustrate his greatness as a scholar and as a caring human being. As a means of communal catharsis, the stories proliferated to an even greater extent following his passing. While some stories may be more dramatic than others, the common theme that emerges is a *kavod habrios* — a genuine love and respect for every human being. He treated every person equally, regardless of their level of observance or their synagogue affiliation.

Modest Beyond Words

RABBI KELEMER HAD a keen sensitivity toward the image that a spiritual leader should portray, and how it befits a Rav to be perceived. At one point, the Young Israel of West Hempstead community decided that, due to the expanding size of the Kelemer family, it was high time to present the Rabbi with a raise. But Rabbi Kelemer, who was indeed a worthy candidate for a salary increase, was unwilling. "There are needy people in the community," he argued. "I cannot accept more money when others are struggling or unemployed."

Similar reasoning applied to the Rabbi's car. He drove what is referred to in colloquial parlance as a yeshivish car, a euphemistic expression for a vehicle that does justice to the expression, "All I need is four wheels to get me there."

In truth, his car could not dependably live up to its mission. The day the shul provided him with a new car — with a snarling grill, long muscular front end, and a rare marriage of the finest in engineering and design representing the zeitgeist of America in the 1980s, aka a Chevy Malibu (for the uninitiated, this is far more entry level than a Ford Taurus) — the Rabbi did not celebrate.

Even the modest Malibu was too much, he felt. And the following day, he drove to shul in his old car.

The *baalebattim* were incredulous. How did he pull that off? Sure, Rabbi Kelemer knew how to convert straw into gold, but not the reverse! The Rabbi matter-of-factly responded that he could not drive around in a late-model car when there were people in the community who were struggling, and a new car is the furthest of their concerns.

One Erev Shabbos in November 1991, as the Rabbi was heading back to West Hempstead from his mitzvah excursions, his car, whose ride had the smoothness of a vehicle engineered by John Deere and was as aerodynamic as the Hoover Dam, finally sputtered its final gasp. (Breakdowns were not uncommon, but usually better-timed than on an Erev Shabbos.)

It was really close to sundown and there was no time to call the cavalry. The Rabbi unloaded his pockets and set out by foot to West Hempstead from Lynbrook, three miles away.

That Friday night, *parashas Vayishlach*, the Allswangs were celebrating a *shalom zachar* for their son, who would soon be named Binyamin. Like every Jewish affair in West Hempstead, it just wouldn't be complete without Rabbi Kelemer's participation. The Rabbi, however, was working his way to town along the all-too familiar Sunrise Highway. (Yet again, in this instance, the sundown highway.) This time it wasn't hot (we'll get to humidity soon) nor was it the kind of November weather evocative of a polar plunge. It certainly wasn't one of those Coca-Cola moments either, with brilliant sunshine.

The air was already drunk with humidity when the dark clouds began rolling in, snuffing out the stars, hundreds at a time. Raindrops the size of small squids splatted against the windshields of the speeding cars and trucks roaring down Sunrise, and in retribution the automobiles and trucks sprayed the water collected on the roadbed at the lone pedestrian with the rain-drenched black hat trudging along the side of the road as the wind blew plastic bags and candy wrappers about his ankles.

By the time Rabbi Kelemer finally arrived in West Hempstead, his destination was *not* his home, which, considering the hour (and probably his appetite) would have clearly made the most sense. The shul had long since closed, and the *shalom zachar* (conducted in the HANC elementary school) was already winding down, but that is where he went so that he could offer his always cherished comments. There was no way that the Rabbi would ever miss a local celebration or otherwise, if he could possibly attend.

With characteristic humor and wit, Rabbi Kelemer, who by this point looked like he had just emerged from the Atlantic, apologized, "I am sorry for coming late. I had to walk quite a distance to the *shalom zachar* — and the police were handing out tickets all along the way, so I couldn't walk too fast..."

The Rabbi's comments were countered by Ronnie Allswang, the baby's father. He related that there was a polemic in the *parashah* as to whether Yaakov Avinu had dispatched messengers or actual angels. "In West Hempstead," declared the indebted and humbled father, "there is no debate that the Rabbi is an actual angel."

Communal Action

EVERYONE IN THE Young Israel community was blessed with an uplifting interaction with Rabbi Kelemer. After his passing, in order to preserve such stories and to memorialize the Rabbi, the community set up an email address, monitored by Dr. Stuart Apfel, to which stories could be sent. Many hundreds of stories were submitted, and thousands more circulate orally. This volume is a collection of personal narratives that testify to the legacy of this great tzaddik who benefited our world. Far more stories than could reasonably be included in this volume were collected. We include only a small representative sample depicting what a remarkable man Rabbi Kelemer was and how he embodied the image of a *tzaddik gamur*, a completely righteous individual.

Dr. Apfel (also a paragon of humility), who was exceptionally close to the Rabbi, felt himself unworthy of this task, hence he wrote:

> *I must ask mechilah from Rabbi Kelemer and his family on two counts. First, I am acutely aware that I am wholly inadequate for the task of organizing this volume and attempting to present a picture of the fullness of Rabbi Kelemer's life. There aren't enough words to do justice to all that Rabbi Kelemer was and did. The best I could do is to let the stories included speak for themselves, with the disclaimer that they barely scratch the surface of the real person and his legacy.*
>
> *Secondly, Rabbi Kelemer was a most modest person who always sought to deflect the praise that he so richly deserved. One year, over the Rabbi's objections, the Young Israel of West Hempstead insisted on honoring the Rabbi and Rebbetzin at the annual dinner. A video was prepared with numerous interviews testifying to the unique tzidkus of Rabbi Kelemer. During the preparation of the video, I made the mistake of mentioning to the Rabbi that even Moshe Rabbeinu had not*

received such praise. It was the first time I had ever seen him agitated; the Rabbi begged me to put a stop to it. He viewed himself as just another member of the Jewish community. I hope and pray that he will forgive our efforts to share aspects of his remarkable life with the world in order that others may be inspired to emulate the ways of Rabbi Yehuda Kelemer.

The Rabbi Yehuda Kelemer story is a perplexing conundrum from every angle. Every aspect of his life not only defies the odds but totally misses the curve. Thousands of great scholars studied in Jerusalem, but not even a handful earned the trust and respect of Rav Yosef Shalom Elyashiv. Thousands of yeshivah students recommend their yeshivah comrades and even their *chavrusas* to date their sister. But how often does a *roommate* ever proclaim that he has the perfect match?

It is nearly unheard of for a Rosh Yeshivah-caliber *Gadol* to accept the position of becoming a Young Israel Rabbi. Even without this mega-anomaly, was there ever a Rabbi more respected and admired?

The Young Israel of Brookline is reputed to have more PhDs than all of Harvard and MIT combined. This probably isn't true, but the assertion is reflective of the brain trust prevalent among the Young Israel's membership. It is understandable that highly educated people are most at home with peers of similar accomplishments. Rabbi Kelemer never attended an Ivy League college, nor did he ever engage in doctoral study. Yet this did not in any way distance this young Rabbi from his congregants, who looked up to and revered him.

CHAPTER TWO

The Life of Rabbi Yehuda Kelemer

Timing is everything, and the timing of Yehuda Kelemer's birth worked against him from the start. Born in 1946 at the time of The Greatest Generation, he was statistically a baby boomer. Just one year earlier, more than twelve million men and women took off their uniforms and rejoined civilian life. America at that time was recovering in the shadow of World War II. More than 292,000 Americans were killed in battle. More than 1.7 million returned home physically affected, suffering afflictions, syndromes, blindness, missing limbs or paralysis. All were battle-scarred and exhausted, eager to put the war behind them, convinced that they had experienced enough adventure for a lifetime.

The lives of women also changed inexorably. Single young women streamed into Washington to meet the ever-expanding need for clerical services, while millions of wives whose husbands had been mobilized learned to drive trucks and handle welding torches. The old rules of gender roles and expectations had altered radically in the working world. It was a new era of optimism and prosperity, and precisely *not* the right time to raise a future *Gadol b'Yisrael*.

But as this volume shall illustrate, Yehuda Kelemer was *l'maalah min hazman* — above time. Bad timing could not impinge upon his iron will.

Maybe the sparks of greatness were not discernible at a tender age, but Rabbi Kelemer's brilliance certainly was. (thirty years later, he was handed a Rubik's cube and, after examining it, he was able to comprehend the algorithms necessary to solve the knotty combination puzzle.) Yehuda was enrolled in the Hebrew Academy of Miami Beach, and the legendary founder and principal, Rabbi Sender Gross, took a strong liking to Yehuda. When Yehuda was in middle school, his father began looking for a new job. Interestingly, the primary consideration for Chazan Berele (Dov) Kelemer was not salary or the community. Foremost, he was interested in the climate, as he feared that his tenor voice would suffer in any place other than a warm climate. Thus, when a position opened up in Los Angeles, the Kelemers headed west.

Chazan Berele and Rivka Kelemer saw to it that their sons had a Jewish education, but the finest yeshivah education that America had to offer was not found on the West Coast in the late 1950s. Los Angeles at the time was not even a flicker of the Jewish community that it is today. The smattering of institutions of Jewish education there would never award the Jewish People with a leader and Torah authority like Rabbi Kelemer. Furthermore, the out-of-town possibility was simply not the mindset in the late 1950s and '60s. The odds were overwhelming that this precocious child would eventually be admitted to a prestigious university and become an accomplished doctor, lawyer or, perhaps, an architect. But, as notably happens in life, intervention by an outsider not only changed the course of history, but significantly improved the future of the world.

The hero in this story is none other than Yehuda Kelemer's older brother Yisrael, who was a student at Yeshiva University in New York City. Yisrael clearly understood that he had a mission in life. His job was to get his younger brother into a yeshivah that would be able to capitalize on the copious talents that the boy possessed. This was a daunting challenge. It entailed, for starters, getting Yehuda to New York — across an entire continent, with no means to cover the travel. It would also entail the significant issue of leaving parents for a purpose they did not seek.

And yet, Yisrael understood that this was his mission in life and that, for a goal so lofty, he had to think outside the box. Indeed, Yisrael landed on a scheme that was as harebrained as it was ambitious. From sources he could never really place, Yisrael had learned that the West Coast winner of the *Chidon HaTanach* (Bible contest) was sent — all expenses paid — to New York to compete in the finals. All Yisrael had to do was convince his ninth-grade brother to study *Tanach* and enter the contest. If Yehuda Kelemer, with his towering intellect, put his head to something, it was a safe bet that he would win. Yisrael was further convinced that once he got Yehuda to New York, he would be able to channel him to a yeshivah without significant parental interference.

Remarkably, this most unlikely scheme worked precisely according to Yisrael's script. The rest is not history, but his story — the story of how Yehuda Kelemer applied himself to the fullest, becoming a saintly scholar who positively impacted upon everyone he encountered.

With stage one already out of the way, Yehuda's avuncular brother sent his younger sibling to the Ner Yisrael yeshivah in Baltimore. Thus, the seeds of a yeshivah education were not only planted, but were already taking root.

The Passover holiday was arriving, which meant a yeshivah recess — but a trip home was unwise as Chazan Kelemer was employed at a

Pesach program, which would not be the ideal environment for an aspiring yeshivah student. Still, the holiday was kept all in the family as Yehuda traveled to his maternal grandparents, the Lifshitzes in Detroit. It was there in the Motor City that his life took yet another unexpected turn.

Young Avraham Mordechai Isbee, who would later become one of the Telshe Yeshivah's proudest graduates, determined that Telshe was better suited for Yehuda than Ner Yisrael. When Avraham Mordechai Isbee made up his mind, other considerations, such as parental input, tuition and other technicalities, were off the table. Indeed, the Telzer actually took the young ninth-grader by hand aboard the Greyhound bus bound for Cleveland, Ohio.

It was only a three-and-a-half-hour bus ride for the young lads squeezed between indigent Americans of every stripe, headed to the bus station in Cleveland, which was abuzz over the recently announced trade of home-run king Rocky Colavito from the local Indians to their archrivals, the Detroit Tigers.

Over the course of but a few short months, young Yehuda went from casual attire to the formal yeshivah world of Ner Yisrael in Baltimore. And when the lad stepped through the doors of the Telzer *beis midrash*, it seemed he had left Black and White Kansas far behind.

Young Avraham Mordechai Isbee was a very religious young man, the likes of which were never spotted in Miami or Los Angeles in 1960. Later in life he would be recognized as one of the *Ge'onim* of Jerusalem, although only the discerning eye could detect the scholar whose dress was identical to that of every other Gerrer *chassid*. But back then, he was escorting a boy a few years younger than himself to a new yeshivah.

Yehuda Kelemer had not yet bought in fully, and Avraham Mordechai's confidence did not dispel the worm of doubt crawling through Yehuda's teenage brain, where images of a rigid, monotonous monastery were taking root. But just as the bus pulled up to the Telshe Yeshivah the highschoolers were out on the field playing the national pastime. At that moment Yankel Cohen, who would become one of the supernovas of Telshe, and was already a star bright enough to illuminate others, hit one outta the park. After his traveling mate explained to Yehuda (who, like most American kids, adored sports) who the batter was and his rank in the *beis midrash*, for Yehuda Kelemer it was truly a home run, and he resumed breathing.

He was diffidently embarking upon a new stage in life, confident at least that he was resting upon the shoulders of his distinguished chassidic forbears. More specifically, he descended from the *Degel Machaneh Efraim* (grandson of the Baal Shem Tov) the *Me'or Einayim*, and some of the most notable *chassidim* from several celebrated chassidic courts. His father descended from the Baal Shem, and his maternal grandfather from Lodz had learned with the Beis Yisrael. Even at a tender age he sensed the onus of responsibility squarely upon his shoulders. Because he bore the genes of these giants, something very lofty was expected from him.

His own deduction was fortified by his father who used to say, "*G'denk, du bist der Baal Shem Tov's an einekel.* Remember, you are a descendant of the holy Baal Shem Tov." This was not a hubristic family password, but a charge and an expectation. Later in life, his grandparents would emphasize the lessons of the Baal Shem Tov, his love of every Jew and constant awareness of God's presence.

But for now, home run legends Rocky Colavito and Yankel Cohen were on Yehuda's mind. When the fifteen-year-old pushed open the door to the Telzer *beis midrash*, the hullabaloo of the last four hours was silenced forever. The singsong of the learning was goosebump territory. It was then that Yehuda heard the rumbling. It was a sound he had known since boyhood, the sound the world makes when it pauses for that fleeting moment while a person decides whether to stand still or leap forward. Yehuda Kelemer, with his chassidic forbears pushing like wind at his back, took a running leap upward and never came down. Telshe would be his new home, and the launching pad for a lifetime of uninterrupted Torah study.

But how would a poor boy manage without any resources? Providence had assigned him a roommate who would look after him and, ultimately, recommend his permanent roommate. But for now, some adjustments had to be made. Telshe was an "Ivy League yeshivah" and Yehuda had emerged from a day school background. With his phenomenal intellect he would pick up the slack in no time, but in that immediate interim he needed some support and guidance. Chaim Walkin, his wise and benevolent roommate, was precisely what the doctor ordered. Chaim would assist with his adjustment and provisions.

For the next few years, when Yehuda was only nominally supported, Chaim was there for him, his bedrock and closest friend. And decades before Rav Chaim Walkin would become revered as one of the most outstanding *mussar* personalities of the generation, he would also become Yehuda Kelemer's brother-in-law. This took place in 1966 in New York, when Rochi Walkin, daughter of the famed Rabbi Shmuel Walkin, scion of a Lithuanian Rabbinic dynasty, married Yehuda Kelemer. After a joyous week of wedding celebrations, the couple was off to Israel, where Yehuda would learn in the Mirrer Yeshiva, preceding the waves of American students who would do the same a decade later.

Why the Kelemers decided to make this nearly unprecedented trip at the beginning of their married lives is not clear, but it fits with the many inexplicable events of this story. Their first stop was a rented apartment on Rechov Hama'apilim that belonged to the foreign ministry and was available for a year, as its occupant, Professor Simon, had assumed residency at his post in Austria. All together, the Kelemers were in four different apartments in the span of three years (at that time it was hard to find a long-term furnished apartment) in Jerusalem's Katamon neighborhood. This was in 1966, when today's popular neighborhoods near the Mirrer Yeshivah such as Arzei Habirah, Ramat Eshkol and Sanhedria Murchevet did not yet exist (nor were their locations under Israeli sovereignty)!

Upon hunting for their penultimate apartment, they found one that met with their approval. No money changed hands nor were any documents signed, but later that evening Mrs. Kelemer decided that the apartment did not appeal to her. Considering that the only commitment that was made was verbal, there was ground halachically and legally to back out. But Rabbi Kelemer questioned with incredulity, "I have given my word; how can I take it back?"

Thus began the wonder years of Rabbi Kelemer's learning immersion in the Mirrer Yeshivah at the feet of Rav Chaim Shmuelevitz and Rav Nochum Percowitz, sitting side by side with the outstanding *posek* Rav Yosef Shalom Elyashiv, who would later comment, "Rabbi Kelemer's rulings may be relied upon!" These three giants took a profound liking to Yehuda Kelemer and were deeply saddened when he returned overseas for gainful employment in the Rabbinate.

The early years of the Kelemers' marriage faced financial challenges. They viewed this as a minor problem, as they were both such spiritually inclined individuals that finances played the smallest role in their quality of life. Still, it was a problem and Yehuda dabbled in mercantile pursuit. It was an ephemeral entrepreneurial endeavor, which ultimately proved inadequate to keep the lights on.

Then a position opened up in the yeshivah in Montreux, Switzerland. Geographically, this seemed to make sense. It was not that far from Israel and, if the plans did not work out, they would be 2,500 miles closer to America. However, after years of growth in Telshe followed by rocketing even higher in the Mir, the Swiss yeshivah was too hard a landing for Yehuda Kelemer. If he was going to make his mark in a yeshivah, it would need to be one with a more committed and advanced student body.

After the disappointment of the Swiss experiment, the Kelemers returned to America and rented an apartment near Mrs. Kelemer's parents in Kew Gardens, Queens. Once there, Rabbi

Kelemer landed his first position in the Rabbinate in Middle Village, Queens. This was followed by the prestigious job of Rabbi in the Young Israel of Brookline, Massachusetts. The president of the Young Israel, Dr. Baruch Brody, a professor of philosophy at MIT, had a connection with the Walkin family and floated the idea.

To say this was a long shot is an understatement. The membership of the Young Israel was exceptionally academic, and Rabbi Kelemer's stellar yeshivah qualifications did not register with congregants so ensconced in the world of academia that rumor had it that on the membership application to the shul, the title "Dr." was already printed on the line where the name was to be filled in. Rabbi Kelemer's predecessor in the Young Israel of Brookline was Rabbi Saul Berman, whose previous pulpit was in Berkley.

It was a given that the Rabbi of Young Israel of Brookline had to be college-educated, with at least one graduate degree from an Ivy League university (although Oxford, Stanford, or MIT would probably also qualify). In fact, Rabbi Kelemer was college-educated. Even though Telshe had an iron-clad rule forbidding college attendance, the Telzer Rosh Yeshivah, Rabbi Mordechai Gifter, had feared they would lose their star pupil if Yehuda Kelemer was not allowed to fulfill his parents' insistence that he acquire a BA.

Ultimately, the Rabbinic search committee,

composed of PhDs in philosophy, mathematics, literature, physics and economics, approved of Rabbi Kelemer simply because these men and women at the top of their fields knew how to recognize a scholar. It was a little too early for them to realize that he was a saintly scholar, but his erudition and engaging personality were readily apparent.

Interestingly, with all the prestige associated with the Young Israel of Brookline, theirs was *not* an eagerly sought-after Rabbinic position. The reason for this, aside from the intellectually challenging congregation, was the presence of three towering Rabbinic personalities nearby. Just up the road was one of the most premiere giants of American Jewry, Rabbi Yosef Dov Soloveitchik, affectionately and respectfully referred to as "The Rav." No matter how brilliant a Rabbi might be, his light would pale in comparison to the Rav's. Picture sitting at the feet of the Lincoln Memorial.

Furthermore, just a little over a mile away was the Bostoner Rebbe, one of the most charismatic chassidic Rebbes in America, who was a magnet for college students. And still not far away was Rabbi Mordechai Savitsky, a world class *talmid chacham* and *posek*. It wasn't all that appealing for a Rabbi to come to town knowing that even in the eyes of his congregation he would always be JV; but these fears did not plague Rabbi Kelemer, a stellar *talmid chacham* who was pleased at every opportunity he had to discuss matters with the Rav, or who warmly felt his chassidic lineage when he would consult with the Bostoner Rebbe.

One of Rabbi Kelemer's first significant Rabbinic challenges in Boston was the insistence of the liberal women of his congregation to carry and dance with the *sifrei Torah* on Simchas Torah. Rabbi Kelemer could not sanction this, but the women were not exactly requesting permission, nor asking a halachic question — they were insisting. A crisis was brewing, so Rabbi Kelemer went to his local mentor, Mr. Erwin Katz. Katz had been around Harvard Yard far longer than Rabbi Kelemer, and he knew just what to do. A meeting was convened in the presence of the well-known Boston philanthropist, Samuel C. Feuerstein. Before the liberal contingent had much of a chance to articulate their position, Mr. Feuerstein, who consistently picked up the tab for the synagogue's expenses, declared gravely, "Rabbi Kelemer is the Rabbi and his word goes. I will have it no other way." The case was closed, and Rabbi Kelemer had weathered the storm.

Although many shuls in America have just one Rabbi with a seemingly lifetime contract, the majority of the Rabbinate is in flux. Boston felt itself privileged to have been graced by Rabbi Kelemer for a full decade. Now the time had come for him to move, and many search committees in America were examining the resume of Rabbi Yehuda Kelemer.

The search committee for the Young Israel of West Hempstead was very diligent in their work. While many believe that Dr. Ronny Wachtel was the key player in this trade, he modestly denies this role, as much as he wishes he could boast of responsibility for this historic *shidduch*. Ultimately, many shul members were involved, as evidenced by the installation (which can be accessed via Youtube) where virtually everyone spoke, other than the Assistant Director of Property Assessment and Appeal for Nassau County.

CHAPTER THREE

The Magic of Making a *Psak* Work

Rabbi Kelemer's proficiency in halachah was legion. No matter what you asked, he knew the answer without hesitation.

Dr. Doni Zivotofsky, the brother of Ari Zivotofsky (of Jerusalem passport fame), and ultimately a large-animal veterinarian, had among his clients the Belmont Racetrack and the Ringling Brothers Circus when they were in New York. While he was a student in veterinary school, he came home to West Hempstead during intersession. It presented an opportunity to discuss some of the halachic dilemmas he faced regarding an aspect of his study regarding neutering.

One would imagine that this is not a facet of

halachah that a *posek* confronts often. But Rabbi Kelemer, without a second's hesitation, replied. "See the *Pischei Teshuvah* on *Even Haezer, siman heh se'if kattan...*"

A *posek* competent in every facet of *Shulchan Aruch* is an asset bestowed very sparingly upon the Jewish People, and commensurately valued. Many people turned to Rabbi Kelemer not just because of his proficiency, but because he always knew precisely whom he was addressing and perceived what they needed — without manipulating the halachah.

Rabbi Kelemer also knew the pressure that a pulpit Rabbi was under from his congregation and the synagogue board, and he knew the fine line one had to tread to remain faithful to halachah and not offend or distance congregants. He had an uncanny sense of when to be firm while still being sensitive and attentive. And, like no other, he had the magic touch to make a *psak* work.

Rabbi Professor J.J. Schacter, who was blessed with a long relationship with Rabbi Kelemer, understood that there was no other address that would be as productive for him in the realm of *piskei halachah*. Rabbi Schacter, it should be pointed out, is no slouch (criminal levels of understatement!) and yet, he would turn to Rabbi Kelemer to resolve halachic issues.

A recipient of Rabbinic ordination from Torah Vodaath and a doctorate from Harvard University, Rabbi Schacter is a noted historian and a full professor at Yeshiva University, the former Rabbi of the Jewish Center in Manhattan, and former dean of the Rabbi Joseph B. Soloveitchik Institute. An invaluable edge that Rabbi Kelemer brought to Rabbi Schacter was that he understood the pressure that a pulpit Rabbi was under from his congregation and the synagogue board. Rabbi Kelemer knew the fine line one had to tread to remain faithful to halachah and not offend or distance congregants.

Because so many people called with their *she'eilos*, and the number was always increasing, it was hard to get through at a reasonable hour. (Factually, Rabbi Kelemer was just not a person who you spoke to at run of the mill 7:00 p.m., for example.) Like so many others, even Rabbi Schacter would set his alarm for 1:00 a.m. to call the Rabbi, who carried (on average) four phones in his pockets, often fumbling to discover which one was ringing.[4]

---

4. The reason the Rabbi carried so many phones was because he would invariably lose one, or its charger, so he would pick up another one. And another. These were cheap burner phones, and just as one phone was coming out of use another was one being commissioned.

Getting on and off trains regularly resulted in Rabbi Kelemer losing or misplacing phones, and the Lost and Found in Penn Station was practically on a first-name basis with him.

In all the decades that Rabbi Schacter phoned Rabbi Kelemer with complicated *she'eilos*, only on four occasions did Rabbi Kelemer not answer on the spot. He pronounced those particular *she'eilos* to be "Rav Elyashiv material," and he would call his brother-in-law, Rav Chaim Walkin in Jerusalem, to present the *she'eilah*. In each of those instances he received word back from Rav Elayashiv within 24 hours.

Rabbi Schacter believed in sharing the wealth and ended up introducing many other Rabbanim to Rabbi Kelemer. A chief referral was the *Yarchei Kallah* that Rabbi Schacter organized every year for communal Rabbis. One year, the *Yarchei Kallah* was scheduled to take place in Memphis with Rabbi Kelemer as its featured speaker. But once Rabbi Schacter learned of Rabbi Kelemer's aversion to flying, and that he was planning to

---

The Rabbi was once on an Amtrak train to Washington DC, and he had all of his phones charging, as he was answering calls throughout the trip. When he arrived at his destination, an amazed passenger inquired, "Are you my senator?"

Hence, calling the Rabbi (even for his children) often entailed trying a battery of numbers. Only the Rebbetzin was usually up to date and up to the hour as to the current number.

The Rabbi, infamous for his adverse driving skills, was once pulled over by a police officer. Even the Rabbi could not imagine what infraction he was violating — he wasn't talking on the phone, was in the correct lane and was driving under the speed limit! The cop explained that the multitude of wires on the back dash (from the collection of phones) had aroused his suspicions.

take a train (a mere forty-four hour ride!), Rabbi Schacter arranged for the conference to take place in Boston.[5] After this assembly, another thirty-five individuals began to set their alarms for 1:00 a.m.

When Rabbi J.J. Schacter's students in Stern College were confronted with thorny questions, he would recommend that they refer to Rabbi Kelemer. With patience and compassion, he would instruct and advise regarding infertility problems, the BRCA gene and a host of other issues that are too weighty for any but the most outstanding halachic authorities.

After these students had phoned Rabbi Kelemer with their *she'eilos*, they would call their professor with tears of gratitude over the guidance afforded and the manner in which they were treated. Rabbi Kelemer never squandered an opportunity to make someone feel good. His broad knowledge and wisdom combined with his gracious caring to make the Stern students feel like they were daughters being addressed by their loving father, with the patience and understanding that a teacher must show a student, constantly displaying a comprehension of their circumstances. Rabbi Kelemer liked to illustrate this with an anecdote.

---

5. Upon landing one time, Rabbi Kelemer experienced such sharp and aggravated internal ear pain, that he knew his flying days were over.

One November day as a high school student in Telshe (Cleveland), young Yehuda Kelemer was focused not on the *shiur* but instead was intently engrossed on the weather outside.

The *rebbi* snapped at the lad, "What's the matter, never saw snow before?"

Yehuda, who had previously spent his winters only in Miami and Los Angeles, answered honestly that this was a first for him. Without hesitation, the *rebbi* sent him outside to play in snow.

Connecting to a Deeper Question

RABBI KELEMER HAD a widespread reputation for being an outstanding *talmid chacham* and *Gadol baTorah* that extended way beyond the community of West Hempstead, across the United States and throughout the Jewish world. He learned with many of the *Gedolei Hador* beginning with his time at the Telshe Yeshiva, and there became very close with Rabbi Mordecai Gifter, the Rosh Yeshivah, who invited him to learn *b'chavrusa*. In the Mirrer Yeshiva, he learned under the guidance of Rabbi Chaim Shmuelevitz, the Rosh Yeshivah. He was also a beloved disciple of Rav Elyashiv for several years, and learned from this *posek* his approach to issuing *piskei halachah*. Rabbi Kelemer continued to interact closely with many of the major *Gedolim* across the world. While in Brookline, Rabbi Kelemer had a close relationship with the Rav, Rabbi Joseph B. Soloveitchik. The Rav would often direct petitioners to Rabbi Kelemer for *piskei halachah.* Rabbi Soloveitchik and Rabbi Kelemer would often be seated together at community affairs, where they would be seen actively engaged in Torah discussion.

It would probably require someone who was a comparable *Gaon* and *talmid chacham* to fully appreciate the depth and breadth of Rabbi Kelemer's knowledge of Torah, yet everyone who encountered him came away struck by his genius, even if they could not fully appreciate its extent. While Rabbi Kelemer's accomplishments in learning are highly impressive, they cannot fully express the experience of engaging him in discussions of halachah and Torah related issues or listening to one of his brilliant *shiurim.* The depth and breadth of his knowledge, and the remarkable way he would tie everything together to derive beautiful and instructive insights, were extraordinary.

The Rabbi had a reservoir of encyclopedic knowledge that he could access in a nanosecond. Word of the Chernobyl nuclear meltdown disaster was revealed on a Shabbos morning in April 1986. The Rabbi — obviously without any preparation — related thoughts from the Chernobyler Rebbe.

This ability became most apparent at events like his public forums, when he would answer any questions posed by community members. Typically, the responses sounded as if they flowed from hours of extensive preparation in the *beis midrash*, with numerous references to sources in an amazing variety of sefarim, some well-known and some obscure, to support his response, all quoted from memory.

It was at the open forum question and answer series where the greatness of his kindness, wisdom and Torah scholarship all came together. In those open forums everyone was invited to ask questions. Occasionally, someone would ask a question that seemed surprising. I remember thinking to myself, "I can't believe they asked that question." Of course, Rabbi Kelemer answered by first praising the question, connecting it to some esoteric question that is discussed in a daf Gemara, and then connecting it to a deeper question, all the while uplifting the person who asked the question. This taught the rest of us a powerful lesson in wisdom, kindness, and how important it is to protect the dignity of others.

One project that was especially dear to Rabbi Kelemer was what he labeled *Kinuss Bnei Hayeshivah*, which he first introduced in the Young Israel of Brookline and continued in West

Hempstead on every Yom Tov.[6] This program consisted of presentations by several yeshivah students who were usually away at yeshivah in Israel but had returned home for the holiday. Rabbi Kelemer asked these students to present a brief discourse during the time that the Rabbi would generally address the shul. Everyone had freedom to discuss whatever they wished, with the caveat they had to leave ten minutes at the end for the Rabbi to speak.

From the Rabbi's perspective, these addresses were a win-win. They enabled parents, many of whom were ambivalent about the wisdom of a non-college year devoted to exclusive Torah study, to see vindication of the Israel choice. At the very same time, they witnessed that their sons had acquired a hitherto unachieved proficiency in Torah learning. Furthermore, the presenters set a good example for younger boys who might have been wavering on spending a gap year in Israel. Most importantly, the delivery strengthened the yeshivah students themselves. The boys were elevated in the eyes of the congregation — critically, the elevation came as a result of their toil in Torah. Rabbi Kelemer felt it was crucial that the boys see that they could impact themselves and others with their *divrei Torah*.

6. Rabbi Zev Cohen, the well-known Rabbi and *posek* in Congregation Adas Yeshurun, Chicago, reportedly was the first participant in the *Kinuss Bnei Hayeshivah* in Brookline.

Well-prepared boys presented their ideas eloquently; others, less so. But no matter what was delivered, the Rabbi never corrected, and managed to extract the kernel of truth that was said or implied. Sometimes this was a challenge that the Rabbi pulled off seamlessly, as he used his ten minutes at the end to summarize, review and recap what was said, extensively praising each one, and then elaborating on each topic, adding comments and insightful questions about various points that were raised.

As one individual noted, Rabbi Kelemer did not so much review what *was* said, but what *should have been* said — all while being careful to preserve the dignity of the speaker with enthusiastic praise for the *drashah.*

> *One time as the Rav was reviewing over the Kinuss Bnei Hayeshivah of the night, he said to one of the bachurim: "On amud beis of the daf in Zevachim that you quoted, Rashi on the top of the amud addresses your question." I was stunned. The Rabbi had been sitting in his seat in shul the entire time. He didn't have a Gemara Zevachim on him to consult with. He was completely familiar with Rashi on Zevachim by heart!*

Selflessness and Tact: Rav Nochum's Example

THERE WAS A PRECEDENT for Rabbi Kelemer's largesse in learning. Rav Nochum Percowitz, the world-famous Mirrer Rosh Yeshivah when Rabbi Kelemer learned there, was considered by countless followers to have the final word in learning. Many wished to consult Rav Nochum or to seek his opinion on the Torah thoughts they had developed. On a daily basis, dozens of students approached him with questions and ideas that they wished to verify as innovative and worthy. Not only would Rav Nochum make himself available and graciously give his time, but he would offer a very special bonus. With unrivaled solicitude and diplomacy, Rav Nochum would comment politely, "I assume you mean to ask..." and proceed to ask an incisive question and offer a masterful answer, incorporating a tapestry of interpretations of both *Rishonim* and *Acharonim*.

Clearly, the person who had posed the question had never thought of such a question nor was he likely capable of doing so. The response was equally beyond the student's ability. Nevertheless, day after day, Rav Nochum continued to implant ingenious questions and answers within the mouths and minds of his colleagues and students. Once, after hearing an entire, lengthy detailed theory supposedly based on a student's query, the disciple himself asked innocently, "I'm sorry, what was it again that I asked?"

Rabbi Kelemer apparently surpassed Rav Nochum's largesse. No matter what the boys said, whether clever, innovative or less so — even significantly less so — the Rabbi's face was adorned with a smile for their valiant efforts and he would gloss over and correct any errors they committed, consistently spinning straw into gold.

One time, a young man referenced a *Gemara* in the beginning of *Bava Metzia* applying the logic of *migu*, which states that if a person has an assertion, he can be believed that he is telling the truth, for if he wished to lie, he could have employed a more compelling claim. An example would be the statement: "Trust me when I say half the lost item is mine, for I could have claimed that it is entirely mine." This argument leads the *Gemara* to explore whether the argument of *migu* ("I could have employed a more compelling claim") is a powerful enough assertion to lawfully extract money. (In the words of the Rishhonim analyzing the *Gemara*: "*Migu l'hotzi amrinan o lo amrinan*? May one employ a *migu* to extract money?")

Chaim, the student presenting, erroneously thought that the Talmudic expression "*l'hotzi*" was referring to carrying (which is in fact one meaning of the word) rather than extraction (a different meaning of the word). This confusion resulted in a baffling and comedic misinterpretation of the *Gemara*, for the Talmud's discussion was not about carrying from a private domain to a public domain, but rather on the topic of extracting money based on a claimant's believability. Nevertheless, from the Rabbi's flattering kudos, one could imagine that Rav Yosef Dov Soloveitchik had just concluded a lecture at the Young Israel! But the best was yet to come. Though the boys would speak on an array of diverse topics, the Rabbi managed in his ten-minute wrap up to tie them all together in a singular thematic masterpiece, as if all the *divrei Torah* were different instruments performing in the same symphony. Imagine tying together talks about geology, astrophysics, ballet, agronomy, fine art, judo and nuclear waste. Not as an improvisation, but as a logical, well-constructed discourse.

The story is told that *maskilim* — proponents of the "Enlightenment" — wishing to derail Rav Yisrael Salanter, removed the *marei mekomos* — the citations that he had posted for his lecture — and replaced them with illogical and unconnected sources. Rav Yisrael glanced at the bogus list and then, on the spot, delivered a splendiferous oration based exclusively on the fabricated sources listed on the new sign.

Only a genius of Rabbi Kelemer's caliber could harmoniously connect what all the boys had spoken about with no prior notice. How he did this was beyond anyone's understanding

— but he did it without blinking. But how in the world would he rectify Chaim's confusion between carrying and money?

Leave it to Rabbi Kelemer, who seamlessly and smilingly pointed out how Chaim was apparently alluding to *Beitzah* 12, where the *Gemara* employs a *migu* recounted in *Shulchan Aruch* 518, *se'if alef*, that just as it is permitted to carry on Yom Tov for food requirements, likewise it is permitted to carry non-essential needs.

Rav Nochum would have been proud!

Pulled Over on the Highway

RABBI KELEMER'S ABILITY to speak spontaneously on practically any Torah related topic never failed to impress. It was as if one could just tap his brain and a wellspring of Torah thoughts would gush out.

> *I remember once sitting with him as he lay on a stretcher in a hospital emergency room, waiting to be seen. He was quite ill, in pain, and feeling very weak; nevertheless, he began to relate an amazing variety of Torah insights, quoting liberally from different Rishonim and Acharonim. The continuous flow of brilliant divrei Torah and Torah related insights was like a fountain of Torah erupting that could not be contained. I would have been completely*

flabbergasted hearing such a steady stream of brilliant Torah insights from any outstanding Rav functioning at full capacity, but to hear it from Rabbi Kelemer under such extremely difficult circumstances, when he was so ill and lying in a hospital emergency room, was truly remarkable!

Of course, what might appear remarkable to most was routine for Rabbi Kelemer. Those fortunate enough to interact with him have many such stories.

At one point, Rabbi Kelemer was giving a shiur to the bnei yeshivah in the neighborhood. The only time slot he had available was, of course, late at night. One such evening, Rabbi Kelemer was driving in the car. So we packed into the shul office to listen as Rabbi Kelemer gave the shiur over the phone. At the end of the shiur, Rabbi Kelemer told us the sources we should prepare for the next shiur. "See Rashi in Massechet Nazir, daf ___, and ___ lines down in the wide lines." After he hung up, we looked at each other, marveling that the Rabbi could give such a shiur while most likely pulled over on the highway without any sefarim open in front of him!

Another small but significant moment:

I once asked the Rav a question about a difficulty I was having with a Rashba in Yevamos, which appeared to contradict the Rashba's teshuvos. Without batting an eye, he referred me to She'eilos Uteshuvos Divrei Malkiel to resolve the issue. How many community Rabbis are thoroughly familiar with Yevamos, let alone a Divrei Malkiel? If only we realized what a Gadol we had in our midst!

There are an endless number of such stories. Perhaps as remarkable as his brilliance and encyclopedic knowledge, was the humble manner in which he reluctantly displayed it.

I was once at a wedding, which the other boys from DRS (a local yeshivah high school) and I were organizing. The boys from DRS were putting on the entire wedding, from soup to nuts. We called them " chesed weddings." This one was a little complicated, with both the chassan and kallah being converts to Judaism. We prepared everything that needed to be done, and things went smoothly until it came time to sign the ketubah. The chassan had bought the standard ketubah at a local Judaica store, but of course, this was not a standard wedding, so the use of the "standard ketubah" was problematic.

Without blinking an eye, Rabbi Kelemer turned over the store-bought ketubah and, from memory, wrote out a new ketubah on the back of the original. In about a half hour all was ready to go. Rabbi Kelemer did it without causing any ruffles, without letting anyone know what was going on, just simply doing what needed to be done. It was truly beautiful to see. The incident illustrated his greatness and brilliance at the same time.

Apart from Halachic Prowess

EVERY BEAUTIFUL FOUNTAIN must arise from a powerful source driving the water to emerge. While Rabbi Kelemer certainly had a brilliant mind, his greatness originated as much from his passion for Torah and its application.

When I was in college, Rabbi Schwalb, the Rav of Etz Chayim, where my family davened regularly, led a group of students from his sukkah to Rabbi Kelemer's sukkah for a simchat beit hasho'eivah. It was a tremendous zechus to join Rabbi Kelemer in that setting and to see him so joyous. Rabbi Schwalb brought to Rabbi Kelemer's attention a halachic discussion pertaining to the brachah of Shehecheyanu that had come up amongst the students while we had been at Rabbi Schwalb's sukkah.

The situation had involved an Israeli man who did not have a religious background, and had asked one of the students on Hoshana Rabbah if he could borrow his lulav and esrog to fulfill the mitzvah. After shaking the lulav with tears in his eyes, this Israeli man asked the student if he could then recite the brachah of Shehecheyanu. Rabbi Kelemer was very excited by the question, and enthralled by the story. He asked who the boy was from amongst the group.

He then proceeded to discuss all the intricate halachic details pertaining to the case, the brachah of Shehecheyanu in particular, as well as the unique position of the Ba'al HaMeor on the topic. Apart from his halachic prowess on the issue, Rabbi Kelemer made the student feel incredible for being comfortable to raise the question, and enthusiastically encouraged us all to engage in further in-depth learning into this area of halachah. It was the way he greeted us, encouraged and taught us so lovingly, and the sincere welcome into his sukkah, that I remember most from that special night.

In addition to his remarkable ability to understand the *pshat* of the Torah and halachic discussions on any issue, Rabbi Kelemer had a unique ability to understand the deeper meaning that many others did not see, especially when it came to interpretations that had an ethically significant message.

A creative ba'al mussar, Rabbi Kelemer frequently extracted gems of inspiration for chesed from seemingly prosaic and often arcane halachic sources. In a responsum (no. 772), the Radbaz writes that a king convicted of unintentional manslaughter is not subject to the usual punishment of exile to a City of Refuge, because if he were forced into exile, the entire Jewish people would be required to live in the city with him, which is an impossibility. Rabbi Kelemer understood from this Radbaz that, by definition, a king worthy of his name must be accessible to his people; he must be halachically able to dwell among them and vice versa. Here, an abstruse detail in a law pertaining to a city of refuge, teaches a powerful lesson about leadership. A true leader is available to his followers and lives in their midst.

Rabbi Kelemer's encyclopedic knowledge of Torah-related topics was not limited to the more familiar questions in halachah, but extended to even obscure topics.

Before Pesach one year, my older brother said he was going to the Rabbi to have him check his matzot. I wasn't even aware that people did such a thing, so I tagged along. The Rav took each matzah and carefully analyzed it, unspooling halachot and pointing out potential problems in some of the pieces. He would say when he did so, 'The bnei yeshivah are machmir on this."

To Make Certain He Had All the Facts

RABBI KELEMER'S BRILLIANCE was not limited to Torah study. One could discuss astronomy, physics (he could expound upon sophisticated topics related to the physics of electrical circuits while teaching a series of *shiurim* on the prohibitions related to the use of electricity on Shabbos and Yom Tov), history (both Jewish and general), English, philosophy, biology and, of course, medicine.

Rabbi Kelemer was often asked complicated questions related to medical halachah. Instead of giving a simple blanket answer, he insisted on first understanding in great depth the circumstances surrounding the question. He spoke at length with the physicians, nurses and any other health care providers who were involved in the patient's care. He also insisted on having a physician from the community on the phone with him when engaged in these conversations, to make certain that he fully and accurately understood the relevant medical details, even if the community physician on the phone had very little to add; Rabbi Kelemer always seemed to grasp the technical details of even the most complicated medical issues perfectly well on his own. Nevertheless, he wanted to have someone who might have even greater expertise present, to make certain he had all the facts correct before issuing a *psak*. Direct conversations with physicians were key to sober halachic assessments.

I was taking care of someone from his shul who was critically ill. There was a question as to whether to do life sustaining measures. I was asked to call Rabbi Kelemer. He didn't want to pasken until he had a chance to see the patient, he said. Rabbi Kelemer came to the hospital to see the patient's condition for himself and only then gave his psak. I have never seen a Rav who actually came to the hospital to see and understand the condition of the patient in order to pasken. His psak was to treat, despite the patient's dismal prognosis. I asked him why, and he explained to me that he is a talmid of Rav Elyashiv, and that this was the psak his rebbi would give. I left that meeting with tremendous respect for him, and I was amazed that the Young Israel of West Hempstead had such an adam gadol as their Rav.

As mentioned, Rabbi Kelemer would typically ask physicians in his community to join him by phone in speaking with doctors and nurses taking care of patients for whom the *she'eilos* were asked. One medical professional notes:

I became very impressed with Rabbi Kelemer's detailed knowledge of medicine, anatomy, physiology, and many other related fields, which I assume he had acquired from years of addressing difficult questions in medical halachah, and learning the clinical details of each situation. In fact, I never fully understood why he insisted on having a community physician on the call at all; it often seemed superfluous to some extent. He always insisted that he needed to be certain that he understood all that the physicians managing the patient's care were saying, as well as what they might not have been saying, so he wanted someone with the appropriate experience and expertise in on the discussion. That may have been his motivation, but in my experience, I found that it was extremely unusual that I was able to provide him with any information about medicine that he didn't already know.

Rabbi Kelemer's brilliance and remarkable memory also extended to other types of feats as well.

During our first year living in West Hempstead, a close friend, Rabbi Chaim Eisen, who lives and teaches in Yerushalayim, had come to visit. That Shabbos I escorted Rabbi Eisen over to meet Rabbi Kelemer. Rabbi Kelemer took one look at Rabbi Eisen and said, "I've seen you before." Rabbi Eisen was surprised, and indicated that he had a good memory for people and was fairly certain that he had not met Rabbi Kelemer before. Rabbi Kelemer thought for a moment and then said, "I remember now. Twelve years ago, I had been traveling in Yerushalayim and stopped to listen to a shiur being given by the Rosh Yeshivah of Yeshivat HaKotel." He then proceeded to recount the content of the shiur in detail. He added, "I remember you were one of the bachurim in the beis midrash at the time.

Rabbi Eisen had been a talmid at Yeshivat HaKotel and happened to be one of the dozens of talmidim in the beis midrash during the shiur. There had been no direct interaction between the two of them then. Not only that, but Rabbi Eisen was much younger then and was clean shaven; now he had a full beard that obscured much of his face. Both Rabbi Eisen and I were astonished at how Rabbi Kelemer could remember seeing him there, not to mention remember in detail the content of the shiur given by the Rosh Yeshivah.

Apart from his wide range of knowledge and phenomenal memory, Rabbi Kelemer was outstanding at applying his knowledge in creative ways, preparing brilliant *drashos*, often on very short notice.

I recall on one occasion, the shul in West Hempstead had to be evacuated just prior to the Rabbi's drashah because of a fire alarm that had gone off. I have no idea what Rabbi Kelemer had been planning to speak about before the fire, but in the short span until the congregation returned to their seats in the shul, he had composed in his mind a brilliant and insightful full length drashah related to the way the congregation complied with the order to evacuate. He compared it to his memories of an occasion when a fire had broken out in the middle of the night in the Telshe Yeshiva when he was a talmid there. He recalled the Rosh Yeshivah standing there and instructing the talmidim: "Leave quickly and quietly." Quickly was easily understood, but why quietly? Rabbi Kelemer was able to derive deep lessons in mussar from that seemingly unnecessary word and shared them with the community.

With a *kehillah* as large as that of the Young Israel of West Hempstead, the ability to compose a *drashah* with little or no preparation time was essential.

There were a few times when right before he had to speak about a bar mitzvah boy or a chassan he would catch me in the hallway (Rabbi Kelemer was frequently in and out many times on a Shabbos morning since the shul had seven different minyanim going on within the immediate neighborhood vicinity), and ask me to fill him in on any more details about the baal simchah than what he already knew. (I'm certain he had many people to whom he would turn for this type of information, and somehow he would always find the right people when he needed them; this was part of his special siyatta diShmaya.)

He would then go on to weave together an amazing drashah related to the parashah, elaborating on the various details I had given him. The drashah was always smooth and cohesive, as if he had spent the entire week preparing for it. It appeared to me as if he had an infinite number of drashos related to each parashah (he never repeated a drashah) and was able to utilize any one of them at will, depending on the situation.

CHAPTER FOUR

Every Student Was Important

After *Minchah* one Friday night at the Young Israel of West Hempstead, the *gabbai* casually mentioned to Dr. Ronny Wachtel, who generally prepared the boys for their bar mitzvah reading, "You know that tomorrow morning, we'll be reading the *haftorah* for *Machar Chodesh*." Frozen in his seat, Dr. Wachtel attempted to ever-so-casually respond, "Of course."

Ronny couldn't believe himself! As a teacher of bar mitzvah boys for many years, at each student's first lesson he made certain to confirm their Hebrew birthday and ascertain which Torah portion and *haftorah* he should help them prepare. For some very strange reason, he had neglected to pose the necessary questions to Gabriel, who was scheduled to read the *parashah* and *haftorah* the next morning. Sunday was *Rosh Chodesh* — and Gabriel had learned the *haftorah* for the Torah portion and not *Machar Chodesh*!

Ronny quickly ran into the *beis midrash*, where he knew Rabbi Kelemer would be davening, and shared his dilemma. The Rabbi told Dr. Wachtel to go to the Gabriel's home to tell him and his parents the following:

There is a tradition among some families of Sephardic descent on the Shabbat a day before *Rosh Chodesh* to read both the *haftorah* for the *parashah* and *Machar Chodesh*. So Gabriel will read the *haftorah* that he prepared, and I will read the other. Rabbi Kelemer will make an announcement tomorrow morning so that everyone will understand why two *haftorahs* will be read.

Once again, Rabbi Kelemer's encyclopedic knowledge and competent halachic mastery saved the day.

Every Question Is Important

ASIDE FROM BEING a world class *talmid chacham*, Rabbi Kelemer was also an outstanding teacher, with a unique style of education that reflected his students' priorities. His goal was for them to grow not only in their knowledge of Torah but also spiritually. He wanted them to comprehend the learning process, excel in their religious pursuits and become better human beings in the process. Many of his congregants had no higher yeshivah experience of their own, and learning with Rabbi Kelemer illustrated how Torah is learned in the most outstanding yeshivos.

During my undergraduate years at Boston University, I davened Shabbatot at the Young Israel of Brookline, and [Rabbi Kelemer] was my Rabbi and guide to the Orthodox world. I regularly attended his Tuesday night Gemara shiur. It was an unforgettable experience. It wasn't just his mastery of the full panoply of commentaries and codes. He was a master teacher who gave us, amid the gray walls of the old Young Israel building, a real feel for yeshivishe learning — something I had never experienced. In fact, he pushed me to later go to Lakewood, for a total immersion in learning. As he put it, "to go to sleep with the Rashba and wake up with Rabbi Akiva Eiger." He was an indefatigable learner, whose quiet passion for lehrnen was infectious.

I'll never forget our weekly chavrusa, from 11:00 p.m. to 1:00 a.m. (and he was only getting started), when we learned all the sugyos related to bein hashmashot and zemanei hayom. It was Rabbi Kelemer who arranged for me to meet and receive my first semichah from Rav Gedalya Felder, zt"l. And yet, these words don't begin to do him justice. He exuded warmth, empathy, caring. He had a kind, captivating sense of humor. He was modest and self-effacing in a manner that is indescribable. He was accessible and available — always. All of these qualities were bound up with his love of Torah, and the fact that he lived in the Torah world 24/7 and brought it to all of us.

Moshe David was Zalmy Kelemer's classmate and best friend. Not only did they spend all day together, on Shabbos Moshe would visit the Kelemers, and on Sunday Zalmy would visit the Davids. To their credit, the friendship involved more than just playing.

One day, their junior high school *rebbi*, Rabbi Pressman, quoted an explanation from the Rogatchover Gaon.

Zalmy suggested to Moshe that they look up the Rogatchover's commentary in his work *Tzofnas Panei'ach*. Moshe was not overjoyed by this suggestion. Although he had never opened a *Tzofnas Panei'ach* before, he knew that it was beyond the scope of an ordinary eighth-grader. It was, *l'havdil*, the Organic Chemistry, Aerospace Engineering, Quantum Physics and Calculus 3 of learning all wrapped up together (in terms of difficulty) and written in a cryptic and telegrammatic fashion. "Nah!" Moshe majorly demurred emphatically, possibly preferring dental work (even sans novocaine).

"C'mon," Zalmy pleaded. "My brother Shalom [renowned for his Talmudic prowess and mental agility] is coming home for Shabbos. He'll teach it to us!"

Suddenly, it did not sound as ominously threatening.

All Shabbos long, Shalom helped Zalmy and Moshe work through the Rogatchover's esoteric words, deciphering his cryptic abbreviations and mastering the abstruse and recondite logic. By the time they were finished, the contents of an entire bookcase were strewn across the living room. Every source the Rogatchover quoted required looking up a dozen additional sources to comprehend the connection and grasp the point.

It was a difficult but rewarding study — and, thanks to Shalom and dozens of *sefarim*, they had actually mastered a commentary of the Rogatchover Gaon.

The next Shabbos, Zalmy Kelemer had an epiphany an apotheosis of a kind. "You know," he said to his best friend, "how every Shabbos afternoon we see my father sitting on the edge of his fully-made bed, studying a *sefer* on his lap? He is learning the *Tzofnas Panei'ach* — without the help of a single additional *sefer*! I guess, after all, he must really be a *talmid chacham*."

Zalmy Kelemer was not the only one to arrive at that conclusion.

I remembered encountering an experienced Rosh Mesivta at one of the premier yeshivot in Yerushalayim, who was visiting West Hempstead for Shabbos. That Motzaei Shabbos, this visitor sat in on Rabbi Kelemer's "baalebatish" shiur, which he gave to community members every Motzaei Shabbos in the beis midrash. The shiur that night was a fairly typical example of this series, in which Rabbi Kelemer explored the deeper meaning of a sugya by examining related sugyos in the Gemara, and explored the approach of numerous Rishonim and Acharonim in understanding one of the difficulties we were wrestling with in the text of the Gemara. When the shiur was done, the visitor from Israel turned to me and said in wonder, "This was not what I was expecting at all. Rabbi Kelemer is a shul Rav; this shiur was on the level I would expect from some of the most outstanding Roshei Yeshivah in Israel. Do you know and appreciate what you have here?"

The Gemara shiur was not the typical structured shiur in which each night we addressed a specific point, which was wrapped up in an hour. It was, instead, the Rabbi sharing with us his thought process as he examined the Gemara and various other sources. That often meant that once the Rabbi had developed his question, he would spend weeks or months following his attempt to address that question.

If the Rabbi copied material to hand out in the shiur, it was important that everyone had the material and that everyone had the place at which the Rabbi would begin the discussion. If someone came late, the Rabbi would make certain that they had the handout and knew where we were, and what we were discussing, before he continued. Just as every student was important, every question was worthy of a serious response. That way he made certain to encourage people to ask questions and made sure that no one felt their question was not good. Sometimes, someone would ask what most of the class thought was a "crazy, off the wall" question. The Rabbi would think for a minute and say something along the lines of, "I think the issue you are getting at is the same issue raised by the ____ (fill in the blank with the name of a distinguished Rishon or Acharon), but he phrased his question as follows…"

That way, the person who asked the question would be left thinking his question was on track. It also allowed the Rabbi to continue the focus of the shiur on the issue he had raised, and not on side or unrelated issues.

The second common factor among the shiurim was that it seemed that the Rabbi was more concerned that we understand the process than emerging from the shiur with any particular substantive point. In the halachah shiur he gave Monday nights, even when discussing some of the most controversial issues, the Rabbi would typically demonstrate that there are important poskim on both sides and provide an analysis of their sources and reasoning.

At the end of the discussion, we had a good understanding of the issue, how a number of poskim dealt with the issue, and what questions the Rabbi had about everyone's approach. We did not necessarily have Rabbi Kelemer's opinion of the substantive issue.

Learning with Rabbi Kelemer was a search for truth.

Search for Truth

IN ALL OF HIS CLASSES, Rabbi Kelemer's goal was to explore multiple sources and challenge participants to re-examine their own assumptions. This style of teaching characterized Rabbi Kelemer and emphasized the deepest aspect of his personality: the search for truth.

The search for the truth meant that some questions remained unanswered. We examined numerous possible answers, but Rabbi Kelemer had questions about all of them. There was no sage in the Gemara whose word was beyond question. Rabbi Kelemer was never hesitant to present an approach from any of the well-known Roshei Yeshivah and then raise questions, never in the sense of discounting what they said, but more in terms of being interested in how that Rosh Yeshivah or posek would respond to the following questions. Raising the questions and examining possible answers was always better than forcing an answer. Rabbi Kelemer always examined a wide variety of sources, and there was never a hesitation to acknowledge that there were sources that disagreed with a position he was taking or even to acknowledge that a position that he was taking might be a minority view among the poskim. Even when just reading and translating something for us, he would stop and go back and explain, "the word I just translated as ___ could also mean ___" — and there would follow a short discussion about why he chose a particular translation.

The beauty of Rabbi Kelemer's *shiurim* was not just applicable to the in-depth classes he gave on a weekly basis. Even the brief *shiurim* given off the cuff for just a few minutes between *Minchah* and *Maariv* were remarkable for their content and insight, despite their brevity — and it is a shame that they were never recorded.

On the day I first arrived from London, I heard that Rabbi Kelemer would be giving a short shiur between Minchah and Maariv. Someone pointed him out to me, sitting modestly at the back of the beis midrash until davening was over. He walked in an unassuming fashion to the front and then proceeded to deliver what I, in all humility, can only describe as a gem: every word considered, measured with so much wisdom contained within it. I remember thinking to myself what a wonderful treat it had been!

Meshulachim (charity collectors) arrived regularly in West Hempstead, and the Rabbi afforded them enormous dignity and respect. He would also ask them to address the shul between *Minchah* and *Maariv* to enhance their self-esteem, which was surely weakened by having to request financial assistance.

Looking to bolster the honor of a visiting Rabbi, Rabbi Kelemer entreated him to speak between *Minchah* and *Maariv*. The guest was flattered, but demurred, explaining that he spoke not a word of English. Rabbi Kelemer assured him that this was no problem as he would arrange a translator.

With this arrangement, the Rabbi accepted happily. At the appointed time, the distinguished guest from Israel scanned the room but did not see any young yeshivah student who seemed to have been designated as translator... until Rabbi Kelemer arose and stood at his side.

Sometimes it was hard to tell if Rabbi Kelemer's agenda was to make others feel good about themselves (which he always did) or if he was interested in empowering others and making them part of the mitzvah process. A Jew, he felt, must be dynamically involved in Judaism and should not relegate to the realm of the Rabbi matters that should be within their own purview.

Prior to Passover, many questioned Rabbi Kelemer about kashering their microwave ovens. Needless to say, this was a *she'eilah* that the Rabbi could answer in his sleep (if that ever happened...) but he would regularly respond, "If you wish to know how to kasher a microwave you must speak with Dr. Lester Pollak." Factually, Dr. Pollak, a radiologist, was very competent to direct people in this task — but the very referral was empowering, which was most definitely on the Rabbi's agenda.

Every Interaction Was Educational

TEACHING, FOR Rabbi Kelemer, went way beyond the classroom or the study hall. In reality, every interaction was educational. So many community members reported learning great lessons by asking him straightforward questions and listening to his response.

I was involved in a machlokes and called Rabbi Kelemer to ask for advice. I asked him if I could tell him some of the specifics involved. He answered, "The most important thing is not the details but principle of loving your fellow Jew — v'ahavta l'rei'acha kamocha, zeh klal gadol baTorah. Focus on the principle, not on the specific details." Needless to say, I took the message to heart and the dispute was resolved.

Even during the holiest day of the year, Rabbi Kelemer had time for a teachable moment with his congregants.

One year on Yom Kippur I realized I had forgotten to light candles. Time got away from me and I was horrified when I realized what had happened. After Kol Nidrei I ran around the shul looking for Rabbi Kelemer to find out what I should do. I was truly panicked, never having forgotten to light candles in all the years I had been married. Finally, I found the Rabbi and explained what happened.

The Rabbi looked at me, smiled and said, "From now on, every year you will light an extra candle on Erev Yom Kippur. Won't it be wonderful that you will have the zechus to be able to bring extra light into the world!" I was so relieved and so overwhelmed that I went home and cried. To think that Rabbi Kelemer saw my mistake as an opportunity to make the world a little brighter. The lesson that was taught to me that night was an invaluable one and certainly one I will never forget.

That Special Yachad Touch

IN 1984, THE National Conference of Synagogue Youth, the youth movement of the Orthodox Union, had committed to create Yachad, a program of inclusion between NCSY teens and developmentally challenged young adults. The model was to be anchored through the Shabbaton celebration, always a core NCSY experience.

We had chosen a Program Director, Chana Zweiter, and under her guidance we began identifying 10 Yachad participants to join with 10 NCSYers and 10 advisers — it meant finding homes to house the chevrah and, more importantly, a community and Rabbi to embrace them. We found it all in the Young Israel of West Hempstead under the guiding trailblazing hand of Rabbi Kelemer. It was

Rabbi Kelemer who introduced the practice of communities around the world to offering aliyot to the Torah to Yachad members. It was Rabbi Kelemer who shared the lectern with a Yachad member offering a dvar Torah to the entire community. I am told it was the first time this participant had ever spoken publicly. And it was Rabbi Kelemer who, in the course of the hours of the morning service, greeted each and every member personally and asked them their names. The Rabbi then rose and delivered his sermon on inclusion and to my surprise, with no notes, looked around the synagogue and welcomed each Yachad participant by name. Many of the Yachad members could not restrain themselves from expressions of outpouring of joy in their moment of recognition. I and so many others couldn't restrain our tears.

CHAPTER FIVE

More Than a Phone Call

There can often be tension between the shul board and the Rabbi, but this was never the case in West Hempstead. Rabbi Kelemer would *pasken she'eilos* and allowed the board to run the shul as they pleased — with plenty of input from the Rabbi, whom they consulted on every matter. There was total agreement between the shul board of directors and their Rav, except on one matter. For years, the board insisted that the Rabbi should have an assistant. They reasoned that there was too much work for an expanding community of 600 families to land squarely upon the broad shoulders of Rabbi Kelemer alone.

The Rabbi never revealed why he was opposed to hiring an assistant, until he confided to one of the oldest shul members, Rabbi Mel

David. "A young, freshly ordained Rabbi," he explained, "will not be endowed with the sensitivity to properly respond to a woman who calls up to inquire [what any calendar lists], 'What time is candle lighting?' Far more than the information, the inquirer is waiting for the Rabbi to call back and wish her a 'good Shabbos.' Nor may the freshly minted Rabbinical student comprehend that a woman who calls up with a complex question regarding family purity desires nothing more than the ruling — not the reasoning nor the various opinions.

"It is the job of the Rabbi to discern what the congregant is truly seeking and address that squarely — and this cannot be delegated to a functionary."

This sixth sense, with which the Rabbi was endowed to perfection, would be missing from a rookie. Therefore, even though an assistant Rabbi would lessen Rabbi Kelemer's load, the assistant would also be a disservice to the *kehillah*.

Also unique was the manner in which Rabbi Kelemer would render his rulings. He never responded with a "yes" or a "no," "permitted" or "forbidden." He would discuss the *she'eilah* by explaining the background and the Talmudic reasoning, but without ever imposing a ruling. After enlightening the petitioner as to the halachic process on the matter, he would allow them to make their own educated decision. People grow from making decisions, but only when they are properly informed.

When the Balabons moved into West Hempstead, a kitchen question arose, sending Rochelle to the phone. Before answering the *she'eilah* (which, ultimately, he never did) the Rabbi inquired, "What does your mother do in this instance?" This caused the inquirer to scratch her head.

After an awkward silence Rochelle asked, "Ehh, how do you know that my mother is right?"

Clearly this question did not trouble the Rabbi, and he said as much. "She is your mother and she raised you. The fact that you are asking me this *she'eilah* today is evidence that your mother raised you correctly. The halachah is to adhere to what your mother does and uphold your family tradition.

Not ever having encountered a Rabbi like Rabbi Kelemer, Rochelle Balabon was having a hard time taking in all of this. At last she asked, "What would you tell your wife to do with such a *she'eilah*?"

Nonplussed, Rabbi Kelemer responded, "To do whatever her mother did."

The Laws of the Torah Are Not Meant as Vengeance

GIVEN RABBI KELEMER'S broad and deep knowledge of Torah and halachah, anyone who approached him with a halachic question, in or out of his community, could be certain they'd receive a brilliant and well considered answer almost immediately. Even individuals and renowned Rabbis from all over the world would often call him for his perspective on complicated halachic questions.

> *He would issue a psak only through clear understanding and familiarity with the situation and the individuals involved. Many times, he advised greater stringency for yeshivah students than for matters pertaining to the whole community, reflecting his consideration of the needs of the community and his belief that full-time study of the Torah should elevate a person to higher standards. His approach to piskei halachah reflected a profound Torat chesed, born from internalizing the words of the Rambam: "the laws of the Torah are not meant as vengeance against the world, but rather [provide] compassion, kindness, and peace to the world" (Hilchos Shabbos 2:3). What others might perceive as leniencies, such as accommodations for the shul schedule or directives to override Shabbat or Yom Tov in the face of serious health risks, Rabbi Kelemer considered as stringencies regarding*

the value of human health and kevod hatzibbur (respect for the congregation).

Famously, the Rabbi favored the side of greater inclusivity, and dispensed wisdom to any Jew who sought his counsel. He was reportedly horrified when one of his congregants questioned the propriety of praying for Jews who violated Shabbos. Rabbi Kelemer's positions stemmed not from an inclination toward leniency, but from his strong sense that *kavod habrios* is itself an overriding halachic concern. Rabbi Kelemer felt the proper application of laws pertaining to unaffiliated Jews or non-Jews was to treat them with respect, generosity, and warmth.

A very well-known Rabbinic leader and mentor once related that whenever he had a difficult question, he would ask Rabbi Kelemer for guidance. Rabbi Kelemer was a fiercely independent thinker who never had to look over his shoulder in paskening she'eilos, and his halachic rulings were always based on tremendous sensitivity to the individual and a sense of realism. On a number of occasions, he would tell me that I could rule a certain way, which might be technically correct, but since it would threaten the peace of the community, it might be better not to rule that way. His rulings were often based on the middah of being dan l'kaf zechut and judging others favorably. If I told him that a certain Rav had paskened a certain way, then his tendency would be to say: "How can we publicly dispute this individual? He's a good person, a yerei Shamayim." For Rabbi Kelemer, communal coherence and peace between disputing parties were the number one priority.

The primacy that Rabbi Kelemer awarded to *shalom* is well-expressed with an insight he once shared. We recite in the evening prayers, "And spread over us the shelter [sukkah] of Your peace..." What, pray tell, is the connection between peace and a sukkah?

Rabbi Kelemer elaborated that a sukkah is a mitzvah composed of many halachic concepts that have no apparent correlation to reality or actuality: There are many esoteric details such as *gud achis, gud assik, shtei defanos v'tefach, lavud, dofen akumah*, and so on. As far-fetched as these principles may seem, they are valid halachic doctrines that enable the creation of a kosher structure fashioned from imagination.

It is this kind of creativity that must be marshaled in the service of peace. The regimented maintaining of a position without giving an inch is a sure way to expand disagreement and avoid peace. To counteract such an approach, our Sages alluded to the spreading and stretching of the sukkah of peace. It takes moral imagination to overlook a slight, and creativity to see good when the appearance is base.

Rabbi Kelemer's acute awareness of differences of custom and context for fellow Jews was remarkable. One year, a boy who had returned from study in Israel asked the Rabbi if it was appropriate to sell actual *chametz* that was stored in the house. Rabbi Kelemer explained the dispensation that would allow for such a sale, but also pointed out the opinion of the Vilna Gaon, which shunned such a transaction. *Bnei yeshivah*, explained the Rabbi, traditionally conduct themselves in accordance with the opinion of the Vilna Gaon. It was now up to the young man to decide what to do, but subtly the Rabbi had already embedded the answer. Rabbi Kelemer intimated that he valued the questioner as a *ben yeshivah*, and the conclusion was now the student's.

Kavod HaBrios in Action

THE OVERRIDING PRINCIPLE of kindness and concern for other people dominated every interaction with Rabbi Kelemer.

> *After dancing the new couple to the yichud room, Rabbi Kelemer, who was holding the ketubah in his hand, noticed a halachic issue with the witness signatures. One of the witnesses who had signed the ketubah did not really know or understand how to write his name properly in Hebrew. With wisdom and*

tact, the Rabbi solved the problem, ensuring that halachah was maintained and that there was no embarrassment.

Honoring Parents and Keeping Peace

AT THE TIME OF the passing of a family member, often, complex decisions must be made on the spot, such as funeral arrangements on a tight timetable. Rabbis are called in and a plan of action for burial is developed in a short amount of time. At these moments, too, Rabbi Kelemer's wisdom sparkled.

A friend, whose parents lived elsewhere in New York, lost his father early one morning. The individual's brothers who lived near the parents asked their local Rabbis whether they could delay the levayah till the next day to allow some close relatives who lived in Israel to arrive, something that was extremely important to their mother. The local Rabbis responded that the man who passed away should be buried that day because of kavod hamet (honor due to the deceased). Rabbi Kelemer came to their home and was asked whether they could postpone the levayah to the next day. He responded that this aspect of kavod hamet is an important mitzvah d'Rabbanan (from later Rabbinical enactment). However, kibbud eim is a mitzvah d'Oraisa —

from the Torah itself — and should take precedence over kavod hamet.

Rabbi Kelemer's wisdom shone brilliantly in many similar instances.

A woman related that at the time of her grandson's bar mitzvah, her husband was in aveilus (the year of mourning). The mourner asked Rabbi Kelemer if he was allowed to attend his grandson's bar mitzvah. The Rabbi ruled that he was allowed to attend, but he would need to walk out once the music started — unless someone invited him to dance, for it would be insulting for him to refuse.

Both grandparents were proudly attending their grandson's bar mitzvah when the music began. As he had been instructed, the grandfather stepped out into the hallway. He didn't get very far before Rabbi Kelemer came after him and said, "I need you to dance with me!" Happily, the photographer captured the moment.

Rabbi Kelemer Knew How to Apportion Respect in a Way that Was Most Respectful

CHAIM AND NAAVA were both from Boston and Rabbi Kelemer had played a significant role in the religious growth of both of their families. Ten years earlier someone might have guessed that one day they would marry, but no one would have ever ventured that they would wish to live the life of a *kollel* couple.

Both families, in gratitude and deference to the Rabbi who had gotten them to this milestone, wished Rabbi Kelemer to be the *mesader kiddushin* (officiate at the wedding). Chaim, who was too young to even remember Rabbi Kelemer, desired that his Rosh Yeshivah be the *mesader kiddushin*, as is generally accepted.

Both families, however — who were footing the bill — were insistent that the Rabbi who was so instrumental in their lives be the one to officiate.

Somehow, Rabbi Kelemer caught wind of the groom's desire, and as much as he always tried to please everyone, he could not easily honor the groom's request without insulting his longtime friends and congregants. His own personal honor was never part of any equation with Rabbi Kelemer.

And then, lo and behold, on the very day of the wedding Rabbi Kelemer — out of nowhere — developed laryngitis. It was a bad case, and he whispered mazel tov in a hoarse, barely audible whisper. Mostly, he didn't speak to too many people as his throat was bothering him so badly.

Surely the groom felt bad for the Rabbi's ailment, but he was also delighted that his Rosh Yeshivah could be *mesader kiddushin* after all.

As for Rabbi Kelemer... he might have considered a career in Hollywood.

You Have No Way of Knowing

SENSITIVE CONTEMPORARY issues have torn apart many communities. Rabbi Kelemer kept his large congregation together with a keen awareness of the role of women in Jewish communal life.

Tension over women's rights is part of the fabric of some Orthodox communities. That never happened here. Rabbi Kelemer always made us feel heard and respected. Here are some examples from his "Ask the Rabbi" sessions that he would hold with the women in the community:

- *A woman asked, "What should we do if we go to someone for Shabbos lunch and they serve us hot soup?" His answer: Wait for the soup to cool down so it is not yad soledes, and then enjoy the soup. The most important thing is that we all go to each other's homes, and not embarrass one another.*

❀ *When asked how we should speak to our children about perversions that they are bound to hear about in the news, he responded, "With kindness."*

Virtually every Rabbi Kelemer story is multi-layered: what was said, what wasn't said, how one would have reacted and how Rabbi Kelemer reacted. The uniqueness of the following story demonstrates not just the trademark Kelemer sensitivity, but specifically the parallels with that of Rav Shlomo Zalman Auerbach, *zt"l*. It repeatedly occurred to this author, who was privileged to know and write about Rav Shlomo Zalman, that there was a similarity of approach between the *Gadol* Rabbi Kelemer and the *Gadol Hador* Rav Shlomo Zalman, evolving from mastery of the law together with compassionate astuteness as to its method of application.

After almost 20 years of marriage, when I considered covering my hair with a sheitel, I made an appointment with Rabbi Kelemer in the hope that he could provide me with some literature to help me better understand the mitzvah. Rabbi Kelemer gave me a couple of articles and told me that, as of that time, very little had been written on the subject.

Nevertheless, I shared my growing interest in covering my hair, to which Rabbi Kelemer responded, "You know that it's very hard for a woman to cover her hair." I was overwhelmed with his reaction. What I expected him to say to me was, "Wow, it's so special that you want to take this mitzvah upon yourself." But, instead, he validated the reality of the decision I had made. I will never forget this conversation, which has impacted so many other decisions in my life.

Compare the above with a story that happened in Jerusalem at approximately the same time: A newly observant woman who had attended classes covering a range of Jewish topics, including the halachic standards of modesty, confessed to her Rabbi that she had a problem. She wanted to observe all the mitzvos, but one of them was simply too much.

She explained that since she had once been married, she was required to cover her hair. Her lifestyle, however, made this extremely inconvenient. She was a career woman and still worked in the same place where she had been working before she became religious. After all the changes that had occurred in her life since discovering religion — changes that had been difficult enough for her and her colleagues to adjust to — she couldn't just show up one day at work with a headcovering. Such a dramatic alteration in her appearance would mandate an explanation, and this would mean revealing embarrassing information regarding her past, about which she preferred to remain discreet.

Her Rabbi listened with understanding to her plight, but humiliation notwithstanding, he saw no solution. The halachah, as he understood it, required her to cover her hair. The Rabbi told her that situations such as this require consultation with an expert in halachah. He would confer with Rabbi Shlomo Zalman Auerbach, he said, and report back to her.

Rav Shlomo Zalman ruled that, for now, she should wear a headcovering for all matters of sanctity, such as prayer in the synagogue and the like. At other times, when her circumstances precluded doing so, it was permissible for her not to cover her hair. The Rabbi who had posed the question suggested that since there were wigs today that looked so natural that few would ever realize they were not the wearer's natural hair, the woman might use one of them. Rav Shlomo Zalman Auerbach looked at this Rabbi for a moment and then responded as only he and Rabbi Kelemer could: "You do not know, nor do you have any way of knowing, how this woman would feel with a wig, which she considers a source of embarrassment, on her head."

With the *Gaon*'s decision in hand, the Rabbi returned to the woman and reported all that had transpired, including his own suggestion and Rav Shlomo Zalman's dismissal of it. The woman was so touched by the Rav's sensitivity that she decided then and there that from that day onward she would cover her hair at all times.

CHAPTER SIX

Under the Chuppah

Baruch's family moved to West Hempstead when he was only three years old. Soon after their arrival, Rabbi Kelemer came to their new house to kasher the kitchen. This was a job that any knowledgeable person could have done and did not require the involvement of a major halachic authority — but that was standard operating procedure for Rabbi Kelemer, who used this service as an opportunity to get to know the family.

Baruch, with all of the maturity of a three-year-old, was amazed to see a religious man fiddling with the dishwasher, which made him conclude that the fellow doing the tinkering was a dishwasher repairman.

A few months later, Baruch was in shul and

saw Rabbi Kelemer for the second time in his life and said, as young children often do, he shouted out, "There's the dishwasher repairman!" This elicited some curious smiles from passersby, and consternation from Baruch's father. Indeed, Baruch could have easily forgotten about the incident, if not for his father's infrequent reminders when he committed other faux pas. Baruch's slip as a toddler was undeniably a classic, but at least it remained within the family.

Two decades later, Baruch was a grown man standing under the *chuppah* on the day of his nuptials and Rabbi Kelemer was called up for a blessing. As he always did, Rabbi Kelemer graciously acknowledged the *mechutanim*, the *chassan* and *kallah*, and the other Rabbinic personages standing other the *chuppah*. And just as the cup of wine was passed to his hand, he turned to the *chassan* and joshed, "You never thought you would have a dishwasher repairman under your *chuppah*, did you?" The groom's jaw nearly thumped to the floor in incredulity, but as it locked back in place, Baruch — still a few minutes away from being a married man — already knew that this was a highlight of his wedding.

Treated as Equals

INDEPENDENT OF MATTERS of halachah, where Rabbi Kelemer was in a league of his own, it was also natural for many Rabbis to look up to him for guidance concerning thorny political problems. Rabbi Kelemer, however, would always insist that the opinion of others, even a very young Rabbi of a small *kehillah*, was as important as his own. He made a great effort to show honor and respect to others, even as they made every effort to defer to him.

I still remember like it was yesterday, one of my first encounters with Rabbi Kelemer was when there was an important halachic and hashkafic issue that affected our communities through a yeshivah that our communities shared. There were questions of shalom bayis within the communities and precedent setting for the future. Controversy was rife and the stakes were very high.

At the time there was just me, another young Rav (also of a small local shul) and Rabbi Kelemer, who were responsible to issue a ruling and settle the matter once and for all. We agreed to speak together on a conference call to resolve the situation. Naturally, my young colleague and I turned our attention to Rabbi Kelemer for his wise and experienced opinion, and we were prepared to go along with whatever he thought was correct.

To our surprise, he refused to speak his mind. Instead, he made it very clear that our opinions were equally, if not more, important than his own! At least 80% of the children in the yeshivah came from his shul, and we had far fewer, but he wanted to treat us like equals in the decision making. I was blown away.

Baruch Hashem, under his leadership we resolved the matter amicably with the integrity of halachah and mesorah, and shalom bayis was accomplished as well.

It was not unusual for Rabbi Kelemer to defer to other halachic opinions that differed from his own.

At one point during the week that my mother was in the hospital, I called Rav Schachter, who was my husband's rebbi, to ask him a halachic question about the medical situation, and Rav Schachter gave me a different psak than Rabbi Kelemer had. I felt uncomfortable about this, as I certainly had no intention of disrespecting Rav Kelemer's psak. A friend related what Rav Shachter had told me to Rav Kelemer, who responded that since Rav Schacter is the Rav of members of our family, we should certainly feel free to rely on his view. I will never, ever forget the degree of anivus in that response.

Rabbi Kelemer often insisted that people asking halachic questions should consult other reliable halachic authorities, especially when these authorities were more in line with the *hashkafos* of the questioner than he was. It was natural for Rabbi Kelemer to put himself and his own needs and ego below that of everyone else.

One year at the annual shul dinner, Rabbi Kelemer, in his opening remarks, publicly welcomed some visiting Rabbis and other dignitaries who were attending the dinner. Following the speeches, I saw an angry shul member approach Rabbi Kelemer, complaining loudly that he had not included a particular individual in the welcoming remarks, after that individual had recently been appointed to some position of responsibility in a Jewish organization.

Instead of pointing out how inappropriate this anger was, Rabbi Kelemer profusely and humbly apologized and promised that he would make certain to welcome this person publicly at future shul events.

Later, I approached Rabbi Kelemer and expressed my surprise at his response. Without question this shul member was clearly inappropriate, and the anger directed at Rabbi Kelemer was clearly misplaced. Why had the Rabbi apologized? Rabbi Kelemer astounded me with his response to my question: "Don't you understand the pain that this person must be feeling inside to act that way? We must respond with compassion."

I learned several important lessons at that moment. I saw the extent of Rabbi Kelemer's anivus, in placing this person's hurt feelings (however misplaced) far above his own kavod. I also learned how important it is to try and understand what motivates a person to act in a certain way, rather than instinctively reacting angrily. This was consistent with his teaching that we don't completely reject a rasha, a person who acts with evil intent. Our obligation is to help him gain a new, Torah-oriented perspective, one that he or she can connect to, that will guide their attitude and behavior in the future. To do that, we have to step into this person's shoes and see life the way he or she does. Only then will we be able to connect to this lost neshamah and guide him or her back. Finally, I learned the overwhelming importance of darchei shalom — pathways of peace — even when it is achieved at the expense of one's own kavod. This was a lesson that Rabbi Kelemer perpetually taught.

Another characteristic manifestation of Rabbi Kelemer's anivus was the great effort he expended in order to avoid drawing attention to himself, especially if attracting attention would detract from someone else's honor.

I purposely davened early so I could spend a good hour with Rabbi Kelemer, walking with him as he made his rounds throughout the community, always elevating the mood of everyone he encountered. It happens to be that on that Shabbos there were several smachot, and he was going to each event to say mazal tov and share in the joyous occasion. First, Rabbi Kelemer spoke at the main shul of the Young Israel after Shacharis for a simchah. Afterward, before davening Mussaf, he planned to walk to another shul in the community to wish a mazal tov to a bar mitzvah boy. On the way, he was constantly kicking rocks and stones. After a few minutes I realized that Rabbi Kelemer was kicking the rocks out of my way so I shouldn't trip on them. He did this the entire 25-minute walk there and back. The walk should have been only 10 minutes, but he stopped to speak with each person he met on the way.

When we arrived, the Rabbi of this shul was speaking, so we waited outside the door so as not to interrupt. While we were waiting outside, a woman visiting from another community came to the door and tapped Rabbi Kelemer on his arm to ask him if this was the location of the bar mitzvah. Without flinching, Rabbi Kelemer answered with a smile on his face. He then asked her name. She replied and responded in kind by asking Rabbi Kelemer for his name.

"Jordan," he replied, so as not to identify himself as the Rabbi of the community (he usually went by the name Yehuda, but Jordan was his legal name).

"Jordan what?" she asked.

"Jordan Kelemer," he mumbled under his

breath, hoping not to blow his cover.

"Oh, I heard that there is a really nice Rabbi in this community named Rabbi Kelemer. Do you know him?"

"Yes, I do," replied Rabbi Kelemer.

"Wait, are you Rabbi Kelemer?"

Rabbi Kelemer remained silent, wanting nothing less than to disclose his identity. Although I knew this was not my place, I jumped in and said, "Yes, this is Rabbi Kelemer."

"Oh my goodness, I'm so sorry for tapping your arm. I heard some of the nicest things about you. I'm so glad that I bumped into you."

Rabbi Kelemer continued to talk with her for another minute or so, making the conversation as cordial as possible, to ensure that the woman left unembarrassed.

Finally, the speech was over, but Rabbi Kelemer still felt too uncomfortable to go in and make a scene before Mussaf. So instead of entering the shul to wish the boy a mazal tov, he decided it was better to leave than make a commotion.

I protested, "Why don't you stay at least and daven Mussaf? You won't make it in time to daven Mussaf back at the Young Israel."

He replied: "I don't want to take away any kavod from the other Rabbi by davening here."

We can detect an identical modus operandi when Yoni's grandmother passed away. Rabbi Kelemer had stood by Yoni all the years as the young man metamorphized from a Modern Orthodox day school student to a *kollel avreich* in the Ner Yisrael Yeshiva — even arranging that the tuition be fully waived. Now, he suggested to the family that it would be meritorious for the grandmother if her grandson were to conduct the funeral.

No one would wish to deny merit for a relative, but it was still an ambitious undertaking for the young man. Rabbi Kelemer assured Yoni that he would walk him through the ceremonial components step by step, and that he would personally oversee the halachic components.

The funeral party was already seated in the parlor, but Rabbi Kelemer was not yet there. Thus far everything was on schedule, so it only made sense to wait a few more minutes — until a funeral home employee inquired as to why they weren't starting. Yoni explained that they were waiting for Rabbi Kelemer, to which this fellow informed him that the Rabbi had phoned and said that he would not be able to make it.

Yoni's shoulders were not yet broad enough to handle the whole service alone, so he was relieved to see a young Rabbi among the attendees. Yoni approached this Rabbi and explained his dilemma and requested assistance.

Just a few minutes later, Yoni saw Rabbi Kelemer standing respectfully in the back. Apparently, the employee had fabricated the phone call, in order to get the show on the road. Yoni bee-lined over to Rabbi Kelemer and apprised him of what had transpired in the last five minutes.

Rabbi Kelemer replied firmly, "Quiet, not a word." He did not wish to intervene in what another Rabbi had already agreed to do.

Despite Rabbi Kelemer's wisdom and scholarship, he would never assert himself in the presence of other Rabbis, unless it was for sake of someone else. That explains why, when he was attending a wedding where Rabbi Aryeh Lebowitz (who was his junior) from North Woodmere was officiating, Rabbi Kelemer gently and politely suggested that the name of the town might be spelled otherwise in the *kesubah*.

Rabbi Lebowitz countered that he had consulted on this very question with Rabbi Nota Greenblatt (*zt"l*), who was known to be greatest expert in this realm.

It was so atypical for Rabbi Kelemer to ever assert himself in the presence of other Rabbis, regardless of his seniority and scholarship, that he called Rabbi Lebowitz the next day and said, "Please forgive me. I just did not want to hear years later that the couple was suffering from a *shalom bayis* [family harmony] issue and a *mekubal* [mystic] will blame it on the way the town was spelled in the *kesubah...*"

Rabbi Moshe Miller was a product of West Hempstead and of Rabbi Kelemer's teaching. When he was being honored by the Yeshiva Gedolah of the Five Towns where he taught, he took special care to see to it that Rabbi Kelemer was not invited. It was soon after Rabbi Kelemer's accident; the Rabbi was very frail and it would have been an imposition that could never have been justified. But of course, that was Rabbi Miller's take.

Toward the end of the dinner, Rabbi Kelemer hobbled in to afford respect to the honoree. Rabbi Miller was crushed with shame over the effort the Rabbi had expended on his behalf. But Rabbi Kelemer, classically, was able to make the other person feel that *he* was the one who was receiving the favor. "I came for my *talmid* [disciple]," he declared, beaming with pride.

The Rabbi possessed the deepest well of honor to afford to others, and he dipped into it all the time. After Aaron Ginsberg, a young man, published a 15-page booklet, he was henceforth referred to by the Rabbi as a *mechaber sefarim*, a published author.

Once, Rabbi Kelemer drove to Toronto to comfort a mourner. It was an eventful trip and there were plenty of obstructions, including border delays, along the way. By the time he finally arrived, the *shivah* was over. Rabbi Kelemer knocked gently on the door and asked to see the mourner. He was unceremoniously told that she was sleeping, and the door was closed. After two days of traveling, the Rabbi said not a word[7] and turned around.

In the Footsteps of Rav Moshe Feinstein

THE NUMBER OF TASKS that occupied Rabbi Kelemer each day is hard to fathom. Harder still is to appreciate how he accomplished them all while paying attention to the smallest details, and honoring every person who crossed his path.

> *I have said many times that there is a certain quality to the talmidim that come from West Hempstead. I often compare this to my friends from the Lower East Side, when we were growing up. I need to explain. Rav Moshe Feinstein was not the type of Gadol baTorah like you have nowadays, where you have husky gabba'im following them everywhere and you can't get near them without some form of protektzia.*

---

7. Heard directly from the Rebbetzin.

Rav Moshe used to go shopping; you would see him in the street or in the store, and in addition to being the Gadol Hador, he was a regular Jew as well, whom people knew and loved. I always felt that this is what allowed my friends from the Lower East Side to grow up frum and normal, because they had nothing to prove to anyone.

They were all friendly with Rav Moshe and his family, so he gave them his stamp of approval: they could be normal people. I have long felt the same way about kids from West Hempstead. There was such a towering, normal, figure of Torah and chesed there, that it allows everyone in the town to grow up normally.

Once Rabbi Kelemer introduced me to speak in West Hempstead, and I began my words by saying this idea, comparing West Hempstead to Rav Moshe's Lower East Side, and Rabbi Kelemer to Rav Moshe Feinstein. My talmid told me that as I was saying this, Rav Kelemer was squirming in his seat, so uncomfortable with my comparison of him to Rav Moshe Feinstein. He was visibly upset. I feel terrible that I caused him pain, but it is the sincere truth of what I believe. When a town has someone so great, it affects every aspect of the town. This is why all the shuls and Rabbis get along so extraordinarily well, which is almost unheard of anywhere else.

Rising to the Challenge

WHILE UNCOMFORTABLE WITH grand comparisons, Rabbi Kelemer never shied away from a difficult challenge. The COVID-19 pandemic presented profound difficulties to individuals and their families. From the obvious health dangers to social isolation to costly interruption of life and income, everyone was impacted. Rabbi Kelemer took this as an indication that he had to increase the ways in which he was there for the community.

Yet, even for Rabbi Kelemer, who was seemingly in a hospital at least once a day, the clergy pass did not carry nearly the same clout that it had previously. Furthermore, his congregants begged him to stay away from hospitals, which were hotbeds of the pathogen.

"Rabbi," Richie Gross pleaded, "this is not just about you. You have a wife and a large family — no one can afford to lose you!"

The Rabbi, who would never belittle a health risk, still looked at matters differently. "Those admitted to the hospital," he explained, "have no one. They are all alone. For some, this is their last day. For some, their very last breath. How can I not be with them?"

And even suited up in a hazmat gear, concealed from head to toe, Rabbi Kelemer was still able to offer encouragement, solace and comfort. That is what his presence always did.

For Richie, that was a moment of demarcation: before and after. Until then, he'd been familiar with the Rabbinic teaching to feel the pain of another person. From that moment on it, was no longer academic.

On a different occasion, Richie questioned the Rabbi, "How do you not get depressed when you hear such difficult stories? Invariably, when people call you it is because they have a trying issue."

The Rabbi's eyes appeared to mist, but there were happy crinkles at the corners as he contemplated, then stated resolutely, "I am a tenth-generation descendant of the Baal Shem Tov. My father used to caution me, 'Yudele, do not forget you are a descendant of the Baal Shem Tov!'

"The chassidic masters taught that one is not allowed to despair. The Baal Shem Tov instructed, 'It will be good, because you will make it good!'"

CHAPTER SEVEN

Like a *Sefer Torah*

While Rabbi Kelemer established personal relationships with virtually every member of his *kehillah* and beyond, he had a particularly close connection with the children of the communities in which he lived. Perhaps this was due to the enormous respect they felt for him, and the esteem in which he held every child.

> *One Yom Tov, my wife had brought our one-year-old son to shul. Following davening, I was trying to figure out how to hold my son and tallis bag simultaneously. Rabbi Kelemer came and took my tallis bag from me, telling me that my son took priority since he was comparable to a sefer Torah. His reasoning was that every child has the potential to become a talmid chacham.*

Behind the close connection between Rabbi Kelemer and the children of the community was the Rabbi's sweet and pleasant smile, signalling his natural warmth. This quickly put everyone at ease, including the most apprehensive child. It might also be due in part to the reverence with which their parents viewed him, as those feelings naturally filtered down to even the youngest children in the community. It could also be due to so many other ways in which Rabbi Kelemer taught, played with, danced with, and got to know the hundreds of children who grew up in the community. The way he would discuss with them what they were learning in school, the way he guided them in the preparation of the *drashos* that they prepared for their bar and bas mitzvah celebrations, the way he would make time for and seriously consider any question or idea a child would approach him with... A high percentage of the community relate the care that Rabbi Kelemer took to never disappoint a child.

> *On one particular Shabbos, during his drasha, my three-year-old son who had been sitting with me during the start of the drashia began to kvetch. So I took him by the hand and we began to walk out so as not to disturb the mispallelim for the balance of the drasha. This is somewhat embarrassing to do as a parent, but a necessity. As we approached the center aisle to exit, Rabbi Kelemer stopped the drashah, and without missing a beat, cracked a joke along the lines of, "Was it something I said?*

Please come here for a lollipop." My son then proceeded up to the pulpit, took the lollipop from the Rav's hand and then we walked out.

At the time, it was a little embarrassing as a parent, but in hindsight it was a huge moment that I hope my now four-year-old will always remember. The memory that this small gesture left on me, my kids and likely the whole kehillah who were present spoke volumes.

That incident was not at all unusual for Rabbi Kelemer.

I was a young child, likely around five years old, and I had been playing outside with some of the other children at shul. I was heading back into shul to sit with my father, when a man wished me a good Shabbos with enthusiasm, and gave me a candy. When I walked back into shul my father noticed me excitedly eating a candy and asked, "Where did you get this candy from?" I cheerfully pointed at the man and said, "From the candy man!" My father smiled at me and said, "That's Rabbi Kelemer."

About a year later, at my brother's bar mitzvah, my father was set to introduce the next speaker—, Rabbi Kelemer. My father looked up at the crowd and related the aforementioned story, adding, "My son innocently referred to the Rabbi as 'the candy man,' and unwittingly, he was profoundly accurate. True, the Rabbi hands out candy to children, but more significantly, he instilled the sweetness of the Torah." This was the sweet tooth that the Rabbi kept bolstering and nourishing.

Honesty with Children

GIVING OUT CANDY was more than a way of reaching children. It was a way of letting them know that their needs were understood and that they mattered deeply to the Rabbi, who claimed the respect and affection of parents and grandparents alike:

One Shabbos when our granddaughter was with us, the Rabbi saw her in shul and wanted to give her a lollipop but happened not to have one on him. He told her that he would get her one. That afternoon when we were taking her for a walk, we met the Rabbi and Rebbetzin also out walking. Rabbi Kelemer was so happy to greet us. The Rabbi reached into his pocket and handed our granddaughter a lollipop, telling her that he remembered that he owed her one.

Here is the leader of a large congregation recalling what he "owed" a visiting grandchild. Promises given must be promises kept — that was the message of the many candy stories told about this great man.

On Friday nights, after my boys sang Yigdal, they cherished the moments afterward when they could go and wish Rabbi Kelemer, "Good Shabbos," and then receive some candy. One particular Friday night, my boys went to greet the Rav, but he had just run out of candy. I told him not to worry about it — but the Rav insisted, asking us to wait a minute while he'd run back to his office to see if he had more. The Rav searched for a few minutes until he found the candy for the boys. I felt bad because I knew that other people were waiting to greet the Rav. Rabbi Kelemer then told me something that left a huge impact on me and influenced how I would raise my children. He said, "It's so important that when you promise a child something, you must always make certain to fulfill your promise. That way your child will learn to trust you and believe you when you tell them something going forward." It left quite an impression on me that the Rav spent several minutes looking for candy just to make certain that the children felt a sense of trust with him.

For mothers keeping track of several children in shul, Rabbi Kelemer's attentiveness to children was hugely impactful. He made sure that not one was ignored, going out of his way to show little kids that they mattered to him, not only to their parents and grandparents.

Teaching How to Live in the Pathways of the Torah

RABBI KELEMER WAS mindful of children's feelings not only in shul, but with every possible interaction. In addition to greeting Rabbi Kelemer following services on Shabbos and Yamim Tovim, children in the community looked forward to greeting him when they came to deliver *mishloach manos* to the Rabbi's home on Purim.

Both growing up as a child in West Hempstead, and later with my own children, I might have many stops to make on Purim. However many stops I had, I always knew that stopping by the Rabbi's house was paramount. Not only for the magnificent mishloach manos that the Rebbetzin always prepared, but especially for the time and attention that the Rabbi gave to each child who came in. He would take time to talk with each one, ask questions, engage in a meaningful discussion and smile throughout.

Even on such a busy holiday, Rabbi Kelemer always made time for his youngest visitors:

We remember when our son was only five or six years old, we went to deliver mishloach manot to the Rabbi and Rebbetzin. Our son handed the mishloach manot to the Rebbetzin and asked for Rabbi Kelemer. The Rebbetzin told him that the Rabbi was not home, he was visiting someone in the community who was not feeling well. Our son was visibly disappointed and we left. Hours later, we were sitting at our Purim seudah and we heard a knock at the door. It was Rabbi Kelemer. He came in with candy for our son, and told us that he had heard that our son had been disappointed to miss him at home that morning, so he was coming to our home to see him. It made that Purim so very special for all of us!

Rabbi Kelemer was a consummate teacher who imbued the children of the community with knowledge of Torah and how to live a genuine Torah-based life with a focus on doing for others. He was very sensitive to their questions and concerns, and understood when they might need someone to explain things gently, even before being asked to do so.

At my Zeidy's kevurah, I was just 13 years old. When Rabbi Kelemer learned that this was the first time I would be attending a levayah, he stood with me, gently explaining all the halachic nuances and customs that were taking place.

The Bar and Bas Mitzvah Opportunity

RABBI KELEMER MET regularly with boys and girls who were coming of age to celebrate their bar or bas mitzvah, asking them what they would want to say to their parents and visiting relatives, suggesting ways they could connect the insights they developed about the *parashah* to their guests and relatives who they wished to acknowledge, and offer their appreciation for coming to their celebration and for all that they do to enhance their lives.

As these youngsters were approaching an important milestone, the Rabbi naturally wished to be involved and help guide them into adulthood. Their arrival at the threshold of maturity was a time to verify that they were heading in the right direction, and if there were troublesome signs they would need to be addressed before the issue would metastasize.

One young man — we will call him David (because that is his name...) — was amazed by how the learned, erudite Rabbi Kelemen could relate to him and his interests, and to the others and their interests — on *their* level. He cited as an example how the Rabbi even figured out how to weave the shoe size of basketball legend seven-foot-one Shaquille O'Neal (twenty-two, in the unlikely event the reader is unfamiliar) into a *gematria* in David's sermon.

This Rabbinic excursus was not performed to demonstrate that the Rabbi could do anything (everyone already knew that, anyway). It stemmed from the fact that Rabbi Kelemer had asked David who his favorite basketball player was. But even without asking, there was so much that the Rabbi could surmise about the youth of his synagogue just by being an "observant Jew."

When David came for the first bar mitzvah meeting, he was wearing a shirt printed with skateboards. Of course, this did not pass without comment, and not regarding sartorial concern. If the boy admired skateboarding, the Rabbi wanted to know why. There would certainly be a bridge that he could build to span from skate-parks to Torah learning and mitzvah observance.

Rabbi Kelemer's determination to meet with all the children in the community despite his incredibly busy schedule sometimes necessitated his going to unusual lengths.

> *I have memories of Rabbi Kelemer as early as my bat mitzvah in 1984. The Rabbi was so busy that the only time he had to learn with me to help me prepare my speech was early in the morning before going to school. I remember sitting with him at his dining room table. I remember how validated I felt because I had chosen a portion of the parashah to focus on that was not the main point of the parashah — but since it resonated with me, Rabbi Kelemer went with my ideas and helped me build a speech around my interests. Afterward, he drove me all the way from his home in West Hempstead to HANC (Hebrew Academy of*

Nassau County) in Uniondale, where I went to school. I remember the station wagon, and how the passenger door wouldn't open so I had to slide into the seat from the driver's side. The passenger window would not roll up, and the wind blew into the car on that cold winter day.

The encouragement that Rabbi Kelemer offered the children in developing their own Torah thoughts went way beyond the preparation for their bar or bas mitzvah drashas. He always welcomed and enthusiastically encouraged any child to approach him with questions or with their own insights on any topic.

When I was nine or ten years old, I remember Rabbi Kelemer giving a Shabbos morning drashah about Pesach and he included the idea that chametz (leavening) can be compared to the yetzer hara and part of the preparation for Pesach is cutting that out. I had a small thought on that dvar Torah, and my father brought me to Rav Kelemer after davening so that I could share my thoughts with him. I had the idea that chametz can be compared with the ego, and that rising dough is like an inflating ego, as the more it inflates the easier it is to sin. Despite my age, and doubtless how busy he must have been even on Shabbos, he took the time to listen to me, focusing only on me, discussing the idea with me for a few minutes, and treating it like it was the biggest chiddush he had ever heard, with a large and very warm smile on his face throughout the entire time. I'm certain he came across the exact idea countless times, but he listened so carefully and discussed it with me, treating me with such respect, despite my very young age at the time.

He left me feeling as if I had made his day by sharing my thoughts. That feeling has remained with me for more than 20 years now. His kindness, empathy and focus on making certain that people embodied the idea of "vachai bahem" — that you shall live deeply and fully in the pathways of the Torah. The reality that the mitzvos should be something you live with, has remained as a guiding principle of my life.

No Fear of Encroachment Upon Another's Field

TEACHING CHILDREN WAS essentially connected to teaching their caregivers as well. The message of the Torah had to be thus translated into different "languages" to suit the needs of different situations in which kids or adults found themselves.

Many years ago, while doing daycare for babies, I realized the need in this community for a program for our two-year-olds, most especially on my side of town, which was not within walking distance to any organized playgroup. I was apprehensive to open anything as I did not want any ill feelings or to be perceived as being competitive with any other local program. I approached the Rav asking whether I could open up a new program. He answered me with a question: "Will you be teaching them Torah?"

I was unsure of what he meant, as I was certainly not going to be taking out physical chumashim with two-year-olds. So I answered him honestly. "Rabbi, I am not sure what you mean... Of course, I will be teaching them about the parashah and about the chagim and mitzvos, but we will not be literally learning Torah.

His response to that was to give his brachah and full support to opening up my playgroup.

From handing out the lollipops he always had in his pocket to his constant reminder about how children's "noise" was music to his ears, Rabbi Kelemer showed how deeply he understood the needs of these little two-year-olds who needed to have more Yiddishkeit in their lives. Thus, he looked at my program for two-year-olds as a "yeshivah," and so he further explained to me that there is no hasagas gevul — no encroachment upon another's field — when it comes to teaching children

Torah. It is with this love and support that Rabbi Kelemer gave me in running my play-group, that I have been able to "teach Torah" to very many toddlers for many years.

Rabbi Kelemer would go to extremely great lengths to rectify even very minor problems, especially when they involved the education of children. Appealing to civil authorities on behalf of parents seeking Torah education was something that he did again and again.

We had an issue with the West Hempstead school district regarding services we needed, and it would mean that my son would not be able to attend yeshivah after spending several years in public school. Immediately, we called Rabbi Kelemer, who asked for the superintendent's contact information. He spent hours going over all the details of the situation with us, so he could fully understand all the issues. Within a few days, the superintendent called us with a positive answer, a complete 180-degree turnaround from his earlier position. All the Torah learning and mitzvos that my son does to this day are because Rabbi Kelemer enabled him to get into yeshivah.

A strong supporter of the Yachad ideal, Rabbi Kelemer had a particularly avid interest in helping children who might be left out of the mainstream, not only in West Hempstead, but wherever they found themselves. Commitment to the full integration of children with special needs into the broader community was a major goal during Rabbi Kelemer's years in West Hempstead.

No gesture was too small in the Rabbi's mind when it came for caring for children — little ones and older ones alike. Each one had needs, and Rabbi Kelemer took it upon himself to help in any way possible, even if it seemed a most mundane gesture.

One morning in August 1992, soon after we moved to West Hempstead, the Rav came to kasher our oven. We spoke for a while and I left him to focus on the blow torch and the task at hand. When I returned a little while later, I found him dressing our toddler. She had come downstairs in her pajamas with her clothes in hand, asking to be dressed. Rabbi Kelemer's unusual warmth and kindness made her feel totally comfortable with him. I, on the other hand, was totally embarrassed that the Rav had to dress my very young daughter. However, he quickly put my mind at ease, telling me that he had a daughter the same age and, baruch Hashem, had lots of experience in this department! My daughter and Rabbi Kelemer's daughter grew up to be good friends and together gave their teachers in preschool quite a run for their money.

CHAPTER EIGHT

I Will Be Right There

When Rabbi Kelemer was the Rabbi of the Young Israel of Brookline, a congregant was assisting the Rabbi to prepare a body for burial. They finished the *taharah* at 1:00 a.m., and the congregant asked Rabbi Kelemer what was seemingly a rhetorical question: Would he be heading home from the funeral parlor?

"Not just yet," the Rabbi replied. He had received a phone call from a distressed mother in New York who informed him that she feared that her son Robby, who was a college student in Boston, was out with friends drinking in a bar. And while there are plenty of arguments regarding the foolishness of such an activity (not to mention that it's hard on the liver), in Robby's case it was really hazardous as he was diabetic and it could trigger a hypoglycemic attack.

Robby's mom was at a loss in the face of this impending medical emergency. In the end, she called Rabbi Kelemer even though neither she nor her son was acquainted with him. The Rabbi accepted the mission to hunt for Robby, just as he consented to any *chesed* activity, requested or self-imposed. Thus, at 1:00 in the morning, Rabbi Kelemer — looking nothing like a college student or regular bar attendee of any shape or form — began to reconnoiter the bars of Boston, searching for someone about whom he knew nothing than his name. There was Silvertone Bar & Grill, Boston Sail Loft, Five Horses Tavern, Bleacher Bar, Porters Bar & Grill, Corner Tavern, The Black Rose, Bell in Hand Tavern... the list seemed interminable. Boston has a significant Irish-American population and it is the college capital of America.

It would take a team of detectives five nights to comb every bar in the city. And there was Rabbi Kelemer, casing the beer joints, temples of the spirit of agave, total dives, rathskellers, pubs, taverns, saloons, roadhouses, watering holes, spots and drinking establishments of Boston.

It is hard to imagine another Rabbinic figure undertaking such a mission — and even harder to imagine anyone other than Rabbi Kelemer who would not be dissuaded by the enormity of the task.

His Mitzvah

ONE YOM KIPPUR NIGHT, as a couple was making their way home from the Young Israel of Brookline, they saw Rabbi Kelemer running in the direction *away* from his home and the shul. This required an explanation, as on Yom Kippur of all days, everyone is particular to conserve their strength and avoid unnecessary exertion.

"Rabbi, Rabbi!" they pleaded. "What is the emergency?"

"It is late at night," the Rabbi puffed, nearly out of breath, "and I still have some patients to visit in Brigham Women's Hospital." Among those patients was one located on the sixteenth floor...

On Fridays, Rabbi Kelemer would visit patients in the UMass Memorial Hospital in Leominster, Massachusetts, 46 miles away. There were no congregants admitted to UMass, so why, someone asked, was Rabbi Kelemer driving for over an hour each way to visit people who clearly were not be members of the Young Israel? Rabbi Kelemer responded that going to see the patients in Leominster was "his" mitzvah. As for the patients admitted to local hospitals in the Brookline vicinity, everyone expects the Rabbi to visit; that is part of the job description of a spiritual cleric. But driving over an hour out of town is not.

While many stories relate acts of extraordinary self-sacrifice on Rabbi Kelemer's part to benefit another human being, even the most mundane acts he engaged in were spiritually uplifting. Each encounter contained a kernel of holiness that uplifted the other person.

> *When Rabbi Kelemer saw you, he would literally cross the road to greet you. He greeted everyone with a smile and a kind word, and made you feel as if you were the closest person to him. He spoke to you as if he had all the time in the world, even though he couldn't possibly. Rabbi Kelemer influenced every person he ever met. It didn't make a difference if you were the Gadol Hador or the custodian, Rabbi Kelemer made everyone feel loved and they loved him in return. Rabbi Kelemer knew volumes of Torah but was modest about his knowledge. Everyone has a Rabbi Kelemer story and they all have a common theme. He went out of his way, but didn't make it seem like a big deal, and he made every person feel special. He made every person feel as though they were the most important person to him.*

While Rabbi Kelemer certainly made the most of every opportunity to perform an act of kindness and aid someone in need, he was never content to simply respond to opportunities as they presented themselves. He actively searched opportunities to care for others, whether this required a major act of *chesed*, looking out for others or just a kind word.

Many years ago, when we were still new to the community, my family and I were away for a day. That day we had a problem with our oil burner, which started releasing some smoke into our house, not causing any real damage, but enough to set off a smoke alarm. Fire trucks came to investigate, and the firefighters took out their axes, prepared to break down our front door and windows to gain access.

Rabbi Kelemer was nearby and saw what was about to happen. With his insightful mind, he realized that the firefighters could gain access to the house by forcing open a window connecting to the basement, and in doing so avoid extensive damage to the house. He managed to persuade the firefighters to do so. They did that and as Rabbi Kelemer surmised, they discovered that there was no fire, only smoke from an old oil burner.

Rabbi Kelemer then stayed and made certain the firefighters did no damage, guarding our house until the last fire truck left. We might never have known about the role he played, since with characteristic modesty, he never said a word to us about it. However, another shul member happened by and witnessed the entire scene. Later, he told us what happened and the role that Rabbi Kelemer had played.

Energy and Enthusiasm

THE RABBI'S ACUTE caring went far beyond material damage to a house. What enabled him to express genuine interest in the welfare of every single person he encountered was a commitment to the mitzvah of loving every person with the image of the Creator imbued in them. One individual who had given up his membership in the Young Israel of West Hempstead to join another neighborhood synagogue recounts Rabbi Kelemer's kindness in his hours of greatest grief.

> *Three and a half years ago, my father passed away. His graveside funeral was going to be held on a Friday in Monsey on what was surely the hottest day of the summer. After the burial, as we were preparing to leave the cemetery, Rabbi Soniker came to me and said, "Did you know that Rabbi Kelemer is here?" I was stunned. There was Rabbi Kelemer with his walker, as he was still recovering from his own accident the year before. What was even more shocking to me was that although I didn't have a close personal relationship with Rabbi Kelemer, he came to the funeral under very difficult circumstances. But that's just the type of person he was.*

It was critically important to Rabbi Kelemer to be present for every person in need. This, of course, was an impossible ambition. On those rare occasions when circumstances prevented him from being where he felt he was needed, he felt genuine pain. Those who knew him well witnessed his physical discomfort when he was unable to help.

I remember one time coming to speak with the Rabbi on Chol Hamoed Pesach, and found him very much on edge. He was having his secretary Wendy frantically call every Jewish funeral home in Baltimore, MD, to find out the time of a particular levayah. When Wendy finally found the correct levayah she learned that it had already taken place. When she told the Rabbi, you could see the tremendous pain in his eyes and body language. I asked him to tell me who the niftar was; given his anguish, I naturally assumed it must be a family member.

He explained to me that it was a brother of a former congregant from his days in Brookline, Massachusetts, who he hadn't spoken to in years, but someone had informed him that the brother was niftar. He was so distraught because he had missed an opportunity to attend and comfort his former congregant at the levayah. It was clear to me that if the levayah had been a little later in the day, he would have hopped on a train as soon as possible and gone down to Baltimore for the sake of a congregant from Brookline he hadn't spoken to in years.

To seek the welfare of literally everyone he met, one might expect his interactions to be brief. As a rule, that was rarely the case. When Rabbi Kelemer interacted with anyone, he never seemed to be in a hurry. One of the most common sentiments expressed by many community members was that he made each person feel as if he or she was either the only person in the world, or at the very least the most important person in the world who Rabbi Kelemer was interacting with at that time.

Seeing him on the street, he was never in a hurry. He made you feel like you were the only person who mattered to him at that moment. He called me recently to get a phone number for a time sensitive matter. But first, "How are you, Jessica? How are the kids?" After getting the number, "It's so good to hear your voice. Your energy and enthusiasm give me strength." Again, just making me feel like I was worthy.

One woman who was not a member of the Young Israel but worked in West Hempstead recalled how he strengthened her in her own hours of need.

My husband, Lou, was in the hospital near the end of his battle with cancer. Lou had just developed a stroke, when Barbara Kahn, who was with me at the time, called Rabbi Kelemer. His words to her were, "I'll be right there.

I'm in Rhode Island but I'll be there soon." And he was there as soon as he could get there. He proceeded to stay with me through that agonizing week and was with Lou at the very end.

Even though I wasn't a member of the Young Israel, that never seemed to matter at all to him. He took care of every detail of the burial for me. He also periodically called me afterwards to see how I was doing and to see if there was anything he could do for me. That was Rabbi Kelemer. When he was dealing with you, he was only dealing with you. Nobody or anything was more important.

The Hardest Hours After Loss

THE RABBI'S KEEN sensitivity to the infirm and mourners, and his commitment to advise and console, were of ultimate importance, despite the cost in time, energy and distractions from other communal responsibilities.

What stands out strongest in my memory and in that of my siblings is the absolutely remarkable way in which Rav Kelemer was by our side throughout the painful ordeal of our mother's illness and passing. Somehow, despite a myriad of responsibilities and hundreds of other congregants to care for, he seemed to be in the hospital with us all the time, sometimes even sleeping there.

David Kesselman related that his grandmother was hospitalized with cancer toward the end of her life. She had a premonition that she would pass away on Tishah B'Av, and as the mournful day approached, her family braced for the worst.

Unflappable Rabbi Kelemer, as always, had a different approach. He went to visit the woman in the hospital on Tishah B'Av, making sure to remove his leather-look sneakers to assuage the woman suffering not only from pain but nervous anxiety.

Rabbi Kelemer seemed to always be available to people in need. Imagine a busy community leader taking a whole night to sleep in a hospital to be near a family witnessing the end of life. No matter how exhausting, it had to be done! Rabbi Kelemer's all-nighters became legendary in the community.

When Rabbi Mel David's mother-in-law passed away on Simchas Torah, naturally the first person they turned to was Rabbi Kelemer. But he was nowhere to be found. The shul was going crazy looking for their absent Rabbi — on Simchas Torah!

Had they only read this book, they could have guessed that the Rabbi wanted to verify that the deceased had the appropriate *shemirah*. Ater trekking to the hospital, the Rabbi's concern was vindicated — and he remained there, performing the final kindness of *shemirah*.

My wife needed surgery many years ago to treat an illness. The Rabbi drove to New Jersey to daven at her mother's kever, and came to the hospital to sit with me during her surgery. After she was home, he walked over to our house on Shavuos, after he had been up all night in shul.

The Rabbi would overcome obstacles to physically visiting patients in the hospital — even if that meant going around hospital authorities. Invariably, this entailed self-sacrifice and an acute presence of mind, and still he did not always succeed...

Dad's final visit to the hospital was in late March 2020. Despite his children begging him not to go to work, he continued to work in his store and contracted the coronavirus. This was during the initial chaotic period when hospitals were overrun, and effective courses of treatment were not yet established. Rabbi Kelemer asked my husband which hospital he was in.

Fearing for the Rabbi's safety, my husband resisted telling him, until the Rabbi threatened to call every hospital in the tri-state area to find out. Rabbi Kelemer did visit the hospital, but security prevented him from gaining access to the room despite his valiant efforts.

Richie Gross related that when he heard that his closest friend's wife underwent a C-section for her baby born at twenty-seven weeks, he was torn: What should he do first? This was a precarious medical situation that required spiritual intervention, and his younger brother (as he called him) and wife, the new mother (whose parents were in Memphis) also needed immediate encouragement. Not able to properly evaluate if he should first go to shul and daven Minchah and recite *Tehillim* or head directly to the hospital, Richie called Rabbi Kelemer.

Rabbi Kelemer answered the question with a question: "Which hospital?" But that was information that Richie refused to reveal. Post-accident, Rabbi Kelemer could not drive and could barely walk — even with his walker.

And yet, the Rabbi, as if impervious to his own situation, was adamant that Richie tell him the name of the hospital. Richie's earlier predicament grew thornier with Rabbi Kelemer insisting on visiting the couple in the hospital. Richie never wished to be disrespectful to his Rabbi, but he could not allow Rabbi Kelemer to subject himself to such difficulty, especially for a couple he did not even know.

In desperation, Richie stated, "I am not telling you which hospital, but I can tell you that getting there entails going over a bridge."

"Well," the Rabbi exclaimed with obvious satisfaction, "this narrows it down!"

Rabbi Kelemer would go to great lengths to visit anyone he heard was hospitalized, even if they were not members of his community or did not know them personally. This included frequent visits to the hospital and to their home as well. Rabbi Kelemer understood that the mitzvah of *bikur cholim* was not only for the patient's psychological wellbeing but could also serve a therapeutic benefit. Accordingly, he spared no effort to visit those who were ill.

In 1994, I had major surgery and was in the hospital for three weeks and was not permitted to eat or drink anything during that time. One Erev Shabbos the doctor wanted to do a dangerous test to see if I had an infection that was preventing me from healing. I insisted that my wife go home to be with our children for Shabbos. I was brought back to my room shortly before Shabbos, and the Rav was there waiting for me! I asked him how he could be with me in the hospital since it was almost Shabbos. He said, "I wanted you to see a familiar face when you returned from the test." I said, "But it's almost Shabbos and you need to get home!" He responded, "You obviously have never seen me drive."

Fixing Our Ties

RABBI KELEMER'S determination to honor each person extended to those no longer alive as well. In keeping with the Jewish tradition of *kavod hameis*, he spared no effort in teaching this to others in time of loss.

One Shabbat morning I came back from hashkamah minyan and my wife told me that the phone rang and the answering machine went on. It was the hospital calling to say that my father-in-law had passed away. I returned to shul, where the Rabbi was davening, and asked him what to do. He told me to get two of my brothers, and we would all walk to the hospital. The walk to the hospital was over an hour, and it was hot. When we arrived at the hospital, I immediately went towards his room, but Rabbi Kelemer said, "Kavod hamet — we must first wash up and fix our ties, and then we can go in there."

We did that, and as the Rabbi was taking care of things, one of the nurses asked me if he was a son. I told her that he was my Rabbi; she then told me that he came every night and learned something with my father-in-law at about 1:00 a.m. Only then did we find out he was learning Gemara with Dad every night.

After they had taken my father-in-law to the morgue and Rabbi Kelemer had instructed my brothers about being shomrim did we head back home. More than halfway home, he told me that he had forgotten something and that he had to go back. When we got back, he asked where he could find the hospital chaplain. Rabbi Kelemer informed him that there were two men near the morgue acting as shomrim, and asked to make sure they got kiddush, hamotzi and seudah shelishit.

Even after his own serious injury, Rabbi Kelemer insisted upon being present to comfort mourners and to honor their beloved on the last journey to burial. His very presence was considered a miracle in difficult places and times. Yet he showed up, again and again

My father passed away on the morning after Yom Kippur at 6:40 a.m. We were somehow able to get on the afternoon flight from Newark to Eretz Yisrael for the kevurah before Shabbos. I was checking in at 1:30 p.m. and my cell phone rang. Rabbi Kelemer was here! Where? "I am at United Airlines Cargo, I was saying Tehillim at your father's aron and I am on my way to the terminal to see you."

Ten minutes later he came into the terminal pushing his walker, only concerned about me, my brothers and my mother. I was never quite sure how he got there. I certainly know he was very busy three days before Sukkos. This kavod acharon (final respect) to my father is something I could never repay.

Nothing was too difficult for Rabbi Kelemer if someone else could benefit from his efforts.

Our grandmother lived in Brookline and was one of many recipients of Rabbi Kelemer's legendary compassion and caring. A wonderful story is told of Rabbi Kelemer often calling or visiting our grandmother, along with other elderly women who lived in an apartment building near the Young Israel of Brookline, on Erev Shabbos. Following a heavy snowstorm, Rabbi Kelemer personally delivered food to his elderly congregants!

Rabbi Kelemer's legendary custom of walking around the community every Friday night following davening and visiting the elderly, the sick, or those in need of companionship, continued from Boston to West Hempstead. Regardless of the weather or the state of his own health, he made certain to continue doing so week after week. The Rabbi's hikes across the community were not restricted to Friday nights. He would also make many visitations on his way home from shul after davening on Shabbos morning. "I'll be home in five minutes," was basically understood to mean at least an hour. This heartening activity was painfully impacted by his own injury, but he could not be stopped.

Rabbi Kelemer was finally discharged from the rehab hospital on a Friday afternoon.

That same evening, following shul, my wife and I had a lengthy Friday night seudah, after which we decided to take a walk. To our shock, while walking around town, we came across Rabbi Kelemer, fresh out of his own very long hospital stay, slowly and with great difficulty, making his usual rounds walking with his walker around the community and visiting those in need of company and companionship.

Do Unto Others

THE RABBI SET such a stellar example of visiting, caring for, calling up and inquiring about others, one might wonder if he extended the same consideration for his own family. We are all acquainted with individuals who are admirably magnanimous toward others but a tad neglectful to their own family. A story should elephant-stomp this notion.

Rabbi Kelemer's grandson, Yaakov Ginsparg, never expected his grandfather to attend his eighth-grade graduation in Miami — a three-and-a-half-hour schlep (not counting car service, check-in, security, boarding, luggage carousel, Uber...) *for one who flies*. But just as Yaakov was receiving his diploma from the Toras Emes Academy, Rabbi Kelemer slipped into the auditorium.

The noted principal of the school, Rabbi Ephraim Palgon, was about to learn one of his most important educational principles that day. As Rabbi Palgon escorted his esteemed guest into the school building, Rabbi Kelemer apprised the principal that he had just arrived by train from New York.

Rabbi Palgon was incredulous. "How long do you plan on staying in Miami?" he asked.

"Just a few minutes," Rabbi Kelemer responded. He had to head right back and catch the northbound train to New York because of a community responsibility. Sensing Rabbi Palgon's amazement, Rabbi Kelemer said, "Yaakov Meir is very special and he needs to know that I would come in to wish him mazel tov."

Like everyone else the Rabbi touched, Yaakov Ginsparg will treasure that moment all of his life. Rabbi Kelemer approached the beaming eighth grader after the ceremony (where he stayed a total of 20 minutes, with a cab waiting outside to bring him back for his twenty-hour return trip), and wished his grandson mazel tov and every other blessing a loving grandfather would extend.

Decades later, Rabbi Palgon still shares this story with his students, claiming that it was the greatest lesson he's ever learned in love and commitment to family.

Yaakov Ginsparg recalls that toward the end of one summer, his grandfather was concerned that some of the boys who did not go away to summer camp would be left without structure, which could easily devolve into an unproductive environment at home.

Rabbi Kelemer therefore started a program in the shul for these boys, seeing to it that it would have all the components that a teenage boy would crave. He arranged for none other than the coach of the Hofstra Pride men's basketball team to oversee their hoops, for dynamic teachers to supervise the learning and, needless to say, generous helpings of Wing Wan's treats.

Already Paid

THE RABBI'S SMALL gestures of kindness were as renowned in West Hempstead as his Friday night visitations. In his unassuming way, he tried every means to welcome newcomers to the community.

Upon moving to West Hempstead, we asked the Rabbi to come to our home to answer a number of kashrus questions. As he was leaving, Rabbi Kelemer asked if we had eaten lunch, given that we were so busy with moving in. He kindly offered to place an order for us at Hunki's, a local kosher pizzeria, since he was stopping there next. We thanked him and took him up on his offer after he assured us that he was not making a separate stop on our behalf. When I went to pick up and pay for the order, the counterman told us that it had already been paid for.

Paying for a newcomer's pizza was a small gesture that went a long way in making the family welcome in their new community. More drastic needs called for greater compassion and presence of mind. Rabbi Kelemer had the secret gift of knowing when and where he could make a significant difference. This earned him the reputation of an angel of healing.

My daughter was comatose in the Columbia Medical Intensive Care Unit with acute liver failure and hepatic encephalopathy. We were told that she needed to get a liver transplant urgently or she would die within 24 hours. I volunteered to donate half my liver (the maximum they would take) as a living donor, and that was the plan we were going forward with.

However, her doctors told us that given the severity of her illness, they thought that half a liver might not be adequate to save her life. Ideally, she needed a whole liver from an organ donor who had just died. At that time, none was available. I remember sitting on a stretcher outside the ICU, very late at night, feeling the lowest I have ever felt in my life, despondent that they wouldn't be able to save my daughter even with half of my liver.

All of a sudden, I looked up — and there was Rabbi Kelemer, like a malach standing in front of me. Why he was there in the middle of the night, and how he found me, I will never know. He sat down next to me on the stretcher and in his gentle, reassuring way began to speak with me.

I don't recall exactly what he said, but I do recall feeling more and more relief and confidence that things would turn out all right. I felt the darkness lift, and then urged the Rabbi to please go home and get some rest. When he finally left, I felt that if Hashem would send me such a malach it was a sign all would be well... and it was.

Just before I was going to go into surgery to donate half my liver, a donor two floors above my daughter in the same hospital miraculously materialized, and she was able to get the whole liver she needed. I firmly believe in my heart, that it was due at least in part to Rabbi Kelemer's intervention baShamayim.

Lifting the darkness of spirit was Rabbi Kelemer's main business. He warred against the shadows of despair and loneliness, especially among the elderly. They needed his company for nothing more than a smile or a caring question.

When I had my knee surgery, I came home on a Friday. That Shabbos, after lunch, I was on the couch in a lot of pain, with my ice packs, pillows, and blankets. Through the window, I saw Rabbi Kelemer and Rebbetzin Kelemer coming up our path. Rabbi Kelemer was still recovering from his accident and walked with a walker. Of course, I "jumped up" to at least be sitting, and we quickly got rid of the pillows and blankets!

When Rav Kelemer came in he said that they were leaving shul and he thought that he would stop by to see me "on his way home." This was about 1:30 in the afternoon and the Rabbi lived a block from shul. I am certain that he made other bikur cholim stops "on the way"!

He then said, "Come, get up, let's compare walkers." We had a race around the living room to see who could go faster! His laughing and smiling made me forget about the pain! I'll never forget how Rabbi Kelemer uplifted me at that difficult time.

Softly Singing Old *Niggunim*

ALTHOUGH RABBI KELEMER was busy around the clock, he always managed to squeeze in time to comfort a person in need.

Rabbi Kelemer asked me to accompany him to visit an elderly woman who lived on the outskirts of the community and had advanced dementia. She no longer recognized her family and we found her to be largely unresponsive, lying in a nearly vegetative state. She had been both the daughter of a chazan and the wife of a chazan. Rabbi Kelemer sat down next to her and began to softly sing old chazanus niggunim from long ago, which might be familiar to her from her youth. The old woman slowly began to become more responsive and the Rabbi continued to sing.

The longer he sang to her, the more responsive she became. After a while she opened her eyes and began to interact with him. Her daughter, with whom she lived, was amazed and overjoyed. When he was done, Rabbi Kelemer indicated to the daughter that he would try and come by every week and sing with her. Here was a man with the weight of the world on his shoulders, who was continuously busy till late at night every day, yet he was willing to make the time to sit with and sing to this elderly woman on a regular basis.

The Rabbi was aware that he was needed for song, for a kind word, or just holding the hand of a Holocaust survivor. Even third-generation grandchildren were shocked to see the depths of his quiet commitment to comfort the aged.

A number of years ago, my grandfather was very ill. He had faced a long battle with Alzheimer's disease, and frequently required hospitalization, often at Maimonides hospital in Brooklyn. The hospital was a long distance from both our home and our parents' home in West Hempstead. But all the grandchildren would visit with him frequently in shifts at various hours.

One evening at a very late hour, I arrived to spend a few hours with my Zaide, of blessed memory, only to find that he already had a visitor by his bedside. Without telling anyone that he was going, Rabbi Kelemer had driven for hours to sit with my Zaide, who had been non-verbal for many years.

The Rabbi seemed so embarrassed that I had walked in and found him there. Not only had he not mentioned to any of us that he was going, but he was clearly never going to mention that he had ever been there. My Zaide was not his congregant.

He smiled at me as he excused himself, but not before sharing with me that he felt obligated to come visit and show kavod for my grandfather, who was a Holocaust survivor. He also thanked me for allowing him to come! After he left, the nurse on the overnight shift told me that he had been there for hours, holding my Zaide's hand and quietly sitting together with him.

Feeding the Baby

RABBI KELEMER'S PRESENCE in hospitals, even for parents who faced emergencies with their infants, was legendary.

> *My husband and I had been living in West Hempstead for a year when our son was born. I stayed in the hospital over Shabbos with the baby. Early Shabbos morning, the nurses ran in to tell me that the baby was not breathing while he was eating. I called my husband and he ran to Rabbi Kelemer, who was already in shul. They called me and the first thing that Rabbi Kelemer said to me was, "Your husband is coming, I don't want you to worry — he will be coming to you, and we are just going to figure out how he will get there."*
>
> *About eight hours after my husband came to the hospital, a nurse came to my room and told us that our clergyman was waiting at the neonatal intensive care unit (NICU). We were confused. My husband ran back to the NICU and there was Rabbi Kelemer waiting for us. He had walked the eight miles from West Hempstead to the hospital. He had tried calling the hospital to get information, but they wouldn't divulge anything, and he was afraid that we would have halachic questions related to the baby.*
>
> *Having him at our side was enormous comfort and encouraging. Never before had*

we seen such selflessness and devotion. My husband and I were beyond words.

He came to the NICU and sat with us and actually fed the baby. After he was finished, we were concerned that he would walk back or have nothing to eat, but he told us he would walk to Great Neck, which was not so far, for Minchah. Later that evening, my husband and I looked out the window, and we saw him sitting on a bench outside the hospital waiting until after Shabbos for the Rebbetzin to come and pick him up.

If a child would be admitted to the hospital, it was standard operating procedure for the Rabbi to show up in the middle of the night and offer encouragement. If the parents were holding their baby, he would practically "order" them to hand over the child to him so that they could take a walk and a desperately needed break.

One of the aspects of this self-sacrificing quality that puzzled his grateful beneficiaries was how Rabbi Kelemer found the time to be in so many different places at so many different times. Hours and days expanded for him in an utterly incredible fashion. Just as long distance was never a deterrent, temporality meant very little to him as well. If there were twenty-four hours in the day, Rabbi Kelemer appeared to use at least twenty-five of them.

One time the Rabbi was very busy with an unfortunate young woman in the community who was dying of cancer and was on home hospice care. I had been offering a little medical advice to the family, so I became involved. One night, the woman's mother called me at 2:30 in the morning because it looked like her daughter was becoming much less responsive and breathing abnormally. It appeared that the end was near. She had a DNR (do not resuscitate) order and the family did not want to take her to the hospital.

I came over as quickly as I could and saw that the woman was no longer alive. Her mother became extremely emotional and started screaming hysterically. Rabbi Kelemer had told me to call him right away if help was needed, but I hesitated to call him at 2:30 in the morning.

But, since the woman's mother was so visibly agitated, I called Rabbi Kelemer, afraid that I would be waking him up. In fact, it turned out at that moment he was getting on a train to go visit someone else.

He came back at once and calmed the woman's mother. He comforted both the mother and the woman's husband, and took control of the situation. With the situation calm, at around 4:45 a.m., he headed back to the train station to resume his initial mission. I don't know when he slept or where he found the energy to constantly be there for everyone in need.

On one particularly scorching Friday night, Rabbi Kelemer asked for a group effort in Torah study on behalf of a patient at Mercy Medical Center.

The group study (mishmar) whose merit the Rabbi had hoped to channel for the patient's recovery wasn't well attended for several reasons: The planning for the mishmar was last minute, Shabbos began very late, and the weather was terribly hot and humid. As a result, I was the only one who was able to make it to shul that night to learn. Since Rabbi Kelemer had told us that he would try and stop by and share divrei Torah with us, as he usually would, I pushed myself to stay late in the beis midrash.

It was around 11:30 p.m. and I was just about to leave, when Rabbi Kelemer walked into the beis midrash and greeted me. With his typical humility, he apologized for interrupting my learning. He seemed as calm as always, although he was clearly sweating from the sticky heat outside. Rabbi Kelemer told me how much he appreciated that I came to learn, and that he would love to talk in learning with me and share divrei Torah, but he needed to go home first. He explained that he hadn't made kiddush yet for his Rebbetzin, because he'd been in Mercy Medical Center with the patient and his family.

It then became obvious to me that Rabbi Kelemer had just walked home from the hospital, a walk that was longer than an hour in unbearable June heat and humidity. Then I remembered that I had seen Rabbi Kelemer davening in the Young Israel for Kabbalas Shabbos. He walked both ways that night, and still greeted me with such warmth and appreciation for what I had done for the choleh, as if what I had done was anything compared to what he had done."

Call My Rabbi

EVERY ASPECT OF Rabbi Kelemer's character was an example of how a Torah Jew should conduct themselves. Rabbi Kelemer never did a mitzvah or a *chesed* to merely fulfill his obligation. Everything was performed at the apex of its zenith, and even if there is no such expression in English, nothing less depicts the meticulous detail that he devoted to being a fully obedient servant of the Lord.

The obvious examples are *bikur cholim*, *talmud Torah* and *shalom bayis*, but no matter how long the list is, it will really never do Rabbi Kelemer justice, as there wasn't a facet of Torah life in which he did not excel and afford his greatest concentration and effort. Furthermore, the Rabbi's sterling conduct demonstrated that there is no facet of life that is not governed by the Torah.

Tom Laverty was the synagogue's custodian. An individual of Irish ancestry, he had a deep affinity for beer, as attested by his girth. Truth to tell, he was not the hardest working individual, but he got the job done, and for this the Rabbi was always appreciative.

The shul members jokingly referred to him as "Rabbeinu Tom," but humor aside, there was no shortage of those who felt that Laverty could be a little more hardworking and diligent to detail.

As a rule, those who find fault are usually vocal about it. Despite Tom's kingly size, he was human like anyone else — and when his pride was hurt, he went directly to Rabbi Kelemer for therapy. Of course, he didn't look at it that way; he was simply telling on those who were criticizing him unfairly.

Regardless, Tom always emerged from his meetings with the Rabbi with his pride intact. Rabbi Kelemer's perspective was not that he was a CEO of an organization (in this instance, a shul) and for it to operate efficiently, all the workers have to feel good about their jobs. Rather, he knew Tom was a decent human being who deserved respect, which the Rabbi afforded him and everyone else in industrial-size helpings.

When Tom's fireman son died, the Rabbi attended the funeral. Tom was the purchaser of the Young Israel of West Hempstead's *chametz* and the Rabbi saw to it that he was appropriately remunerated for his nominal efforts. And when Tom was in the hospital for what turned out to be his final ailment, the hospital broke the news that it was time to call his priest for the last rites.

"Nothin' doin'," Tom Laverty pronounced. "Don't call my priest, call my Rabbi!"

"But, umm, uhhh," the social worker stammered, incredulous. "You're not even Jewish!"

Like one of the 1960s ads proclaiming, "You don't have to be Jewish to love Levy's real Jewish rye," Tom retorted, "It doesn't matter; I need my Rabbi!"

Remarkably, history repeated itself. Tom's daughter Jennifer was diagnosed with a medical condition that did not have a clear path for the most efficient cure. The ailment was treatable, but each method contained a different drawback and risk. The specialist, a Jewish surgeon from the Five Towns, laid out the options. Jennifer took the notes and then responded, "I have to ask my Rabbi."

It was a family tradition and it served her well. Rabbi Kelemer was very attentive and, with his incisive mind, advised her as to the best possible option.

And Lived to Tell the Tale

MONDAY, DECEMBER 12, 2016, was a relatively regular day in West Hempstead. *Minchah* and *Maariv* had already adjourned over two hours earlier, and the Rabbi was making his way across Hempstead Avenue, the busy street upon which the Young Israel is situated. Unbeknownst to the Rabbi — or anyone else, as the street was oddly trafficless at 7:35 PM — a white Dodge Ram pickup truck was barreling southward. The forty-six-year-old driver, Benitez Rodolfo, an illegal immigrant, was paying as much attention to the road as he was to safety regulations such as a valid driver's license, speed limit and never abandoning the scene of an accident.

And... *wham*! Rabbi Kelemer, who was crossing the street to the shul, was thrown thirty-five feet.

It was an uneven matchup between the lean seventy-one-year-old Rabbi and the 702-horsepower, 560-pound-to-foot torque full-throttle truck. Rabbi Kelemer sustained severe head injuries and a cracked hip and pelvis. Still conscious, but totally non-mobile, he lay all alone on Hempstead Avenue.

The driver was long gone, the Rabbi's plight giving him even greater incentive to speed away from the scene of the crime. The shul security camera caught but a glimpse of the vehicle. Rodolfo would lie low for a while — but when he resurfaced, the Nassau County police, who took this investigation very seriously, would nab him.

Meanwhile, back on Hempstead Avenue, the unusually empty thoroughfare took only seconds to recalibrate. Hardened New Yorkers, as far as generalizations go, do not veer from their path. There is a distinct reason that the "Kitty Genovese case" happened in Gotham and not in Idaho. If there is something on the road, the average metropolitan driver steers around it and stays focused on himself.

But that was not the mindset of the oncoming driver. A nurse by profession, Sophia Dawkins took in what had happened and what might yet occur if she did not act swiftly. She stopped her car and waved cars around the casualty. Finally, people stopped and were about to clear the victim off the roadway, until Sophia intervened.

"He has sustained bone injuries," the Heaven-sent medical practitioner insisted, "and moving him will only make things worse."

Sophia also had to put out a cry for help. She found the Rabbi's cell phone and quick-thinkingly called the last person that he had had a conversation with, Michael Levine. As Michael set about notifying Hatzalah, he asked his wife Simcha to notify the Rebbetzin.

Hatzalah, as always, instantly arrived at the scene — only to discover that the victim was none other than the *Mara d'Asra*. Sirens started blaring like there was no tomorrow, as Rabbi Kelemer was delicately rushed to Winthrop Hospital in Mineola, Long Island.

Rebbetzin Kelemer, living but three short blocks from the shul, heard the commotion, but knew the demon's shriek of sirens on Hempstead Avenue was not unusual. She had just finished informing a visitor from Israel that the Rabbi was not home, when Simcha raced up to her door, looking, shall we say, very un-*simchah*-dik. Her carefully chosen words were, "The Rabbi was involved in an accident." She did *not* say that he had been hit by a truck.

At first, news of the Rabbi being involved in an accident was partially misunderstood. This was the day that Rochi Kelemer had always feared. Her husband's poor driving, coupled with the hardly roadworthy vehicles he drove, were the kind of combination that was mega accident prone. The odds seemed overwhelming that the Rabbi would be the *cause* of an accident (and the fact that this never happened is manifest proof of the Heavenly protection that he enjoyed). Mrs. Levine was spared the necessity for full elaboration by driving the Rebbetzin to Winthrop.

Straight away, Hatzalah radios began to squawk that Rabbi Kelemer had been seriously injured and had been admitted to trauma in Winthrop. Suddenly NYU Winthrop Hospital was atwitter for this Level One Trauma. As the Rebbetzin described it, "The place began to get busy." If ever there was an understatement!

The number of medical personnel streaming through the doors in their doctor's coats, civilian clothing, scrubs and hastily thrown on polo shirts made John F. Kennedy Airport on Thanksgiving Eve look like a Tonka toy. West Hempstead has no shortage of medical specialists, and if they could in any way be of help to a short-staffed hospital charged with the care of their Rabbi, they were not about to monitor events from the leisure of their phones. There were enough doctors buzzing around to have effectively treated the Johnstown Flood, with enough left over to fill the right field bleachers in Yankee stadium. Think of a medical elephant walk and you'll get the drift.

As Rabbi Kelemer was being prepped for delicate surgery to arrest the internal bleeding, consultations were hastily conducted as to who would be the finest members to compose the 20-person trauma team. Among those available were the most accomplished surgeons and neurological specialists in the region. From a strictly statistical and medical perspective, had the Rabbi been taken to a community hospital, he would not have made it. (One member of the surgical team recalled that the week of Rabbi Kelemer's accident, a young man fell off the top of a telescoping ladder in Home Depot. The CT skull scans of this young man and of Rabbi Kelemer were almost identical. Tragically, the young man died within the day, while Rabbi Kelemer ultimately emerged without a scratch to his head.)

With enough medical firepower to take on NIH and Mayo Clinic together, Rabbi Kelemer, attached to a ventilator and surrounded by dripping plasma bags, plastic tubes snaking in and out of his body and blinking monitors, was wheeled through a chevron of doctors into lengthy emergency surgery.

Several doctors in Winthrop, including attending physicians, were members of the Young Israel — and, as a result of the medical influx at the time of the Rabbi's admission, Winthrop imposed no restrictions on the Kelemer family, allowing them to come and go in the ICU as they pleased.

Rebbetzin Kelemer, at her very first opportunity, went to daven at the *kever* (graveside) of Bubbe Mishket, renowned as a *tzadeikes*, a saintly woman. This family matriarch was Rabbi

Kelemer's paternal grandmother (née Gutman). Bubbe Mishket was the daughter of Rabbinic luminaries, a direct eighth-generation descendant of the Baal Shem Tov and a genius in her own right, who knew all of *Tanach* by heart. Rebbetzin Kelemer returned from the cemetery to her husband's bedside and related where she had been. Despite the Rabbi's comatose state, Rebbetzin Kelemer was confident that he understood what she had said and was content.

Bubbe Mishket was a favorite conduit of the Kelemer family. When Rabbi Kelemer's brother Yisrael (of *Chidon HaTanach* get-him-to-New York-and-from-there-to-yeshivah fame) was diagnosed with a tumor in his abdomen, his younger brother went to Bubbe Mishket's *kever* to daven. The subsequent scan was totally clean!

The Young Israel rallied to the aid of the Rabbi by reciting *Tehillim* and accepting upon themselves a host of extra mitzvos and learning. The Rabbi's large family formed a schedule of shifts to be at their father's bedside. Reb Shalom Kelemer was on duty late at night and would walk around the bed learning with a soft, melodious tune from a large *Gemara* with his still-silent *chavrusa* (study partner). Unbeknownst to Reb Shalom, this wondrous sight astounded those awake at that late hour, and several would stop what they were doing just to behold a sight loftier than anything they had ever imagined.

The Young Israel community continued to storm the Gates of Heaven until the first night of Chanukah, when a miracle occurred and the Rabbi awoke from his deep coma. Somehow, all of his precious wisdom was preserved intact and the brilliant mind that reveled in the Lord's Torah was not impacted. The rest of his body was the worse for wear — but the miracles, like waves at high tide, kept washing ashore.

Not just any hospital, and not just any orthopedic surgeon, could accomplish the requisite repair job. Indeed, even a specialist might not be adequately skilled because of the all-important experience-factor, which is so rare.

Winthrop Hospital was blessed with just the right expert. It was beyond man's ken that post-surgery, Rabbi Kelemer would be able to make his way around with the aid of a walker. It deserves a place in the annals of "incredible but true" that nine months later he was self-ambulatory. And to push the incredulity envelope into the stratosphere, with time, the Rabbi's recovery was so complete you could barely detect that he ever had been injured.

In light of Winthrop's relaxed visitation policies when it came to Rabbi Kelemer, Young Israel members anxious to do something — *anything* — for their Rabbi, brought copious quantities of gourmet dishes to the hospital. The staff, who had never seen anything like this, marveled, "Do you guys cook in your cars?"

Between the surgery and the ability to walk was the important chapter of Kessler Institute for Rehabilitation in West Orange, New Jersey. Entering Kessler, one is greeted by enlarged photographs of one of their graduates: Christopher Reeve, aka Superman. The real supermen and women are the dedicated staff at Kessler, who perform nearly unimaginable wonders. Dr. Steven Kirshblum headed the team assigned to Rabbi Kelemer, who taught him in real time and in real life the *mussar* principle that *ein davar ha'omeid bifnei haratzon* — nothing can stand in the way of one's will.

One might have argued that Rabbi Kelemer was already a student of this doctrine, but he claimed that he gained much from this new "*beis midrash*." The Rabbi was always incorporating new lessons, and here is one that he felt so worthy, that he shared it with his congregation:

Dear Member,

I would like to share with you an event in the rehab that has taught me a great lesson. From the first day I arrived, all the way at the end of my floor a woman would cry all night, nonstop, until 6:00 a.m. (apparently that's when she grew exhausted and no longer had the strength to weep). She could be heard clearly across the entire floor. The nurses treated her with much kindness, knowing that she had a brain injury.

The last few days, I didn't hear her cry. I kept asking around and no one knew why. Yesterday I spoke with her nurse, who told me that this patient was rushed to a local hospital because of a severe heart condition and she passed away.

I miss the bechiyah (crying) and am pained that I did not visit her. I learned from this patient what the Talmud says: The gates of tears are never sealed. During the long and quiet nights, I now pray to the Ribbono shel Olam that she should find peace with the Almighty and that He should count all the tears of those who suffer, and finally open the gates of healing and joy for all cholim, without exception.

Rabbi Yehuda Kelemer

The Rabbi had recuperated significantly by the time the shul's sixty-third annual dinner rolled around. There was a consensus that the Rabbi should be the guest of honor. Rabbi Kelemer was as interested in this as he was in a new car, but he did have a better idea and was very insistent about it. "Don't honor me," he declared, "honor Sophia Dawkins!" (Sophia Dawkins was the nurse who had stopped traffic and summoned help for the accident victim sprawled on the road.)

for the home of a family but didn't even know their full name. Apparently, he'd heard that the family was in the middle of a marriage separation and the Rav needed to make himself available to them, even on the Seder night.

Weather or Not

RABBI KELEMER'S DEDICATION to the welfare of others extended far beyond the vagaries of weather. Winter's bitter bite had no power to deter this community leader who was driven to be present at all times. A young man witnessed this phenomenon in January 2018, shortly after the Rabbi began his recovery from the hit and run accident that slowed him down temporarily, but didn't stop him.

It was a snowy and icy January morning, and a friend of mine had an aufruf at the HANC ECC (Hebrew Academy of Nassau County Early Child Center), a shul roughly a mile away from the Rav's house. This friend did not attend the Young Israel regularly, but did come on occasion. I'll never forget seeing the image of the Rav and Rebbetzin with the Rav's walker trudging along Hempstead Avenue towards the ECC. I noticed that there was ice everywhere, and I tried to direct him to the safest path. He did not want my help, but insisted he was fine.

And then, like mushrooms sprouting after a rain in the forest, the idea crystallized to honor *all* of the hospital employes involved in the Rabbi's recovery, starting with Winthrop's CEO. These hardworking men and women had never been acknowledged in a fashion even remotely similar for their decades of selfless dedication. The honorees went home with a beautifully framed piece of art with a Hebrew quotation and English rendition in calligraphy crediting their heroic role. Each honoree's living room is now adorned with what is surely a conversation piece.

The Rabbi's vision of demonstrating gratitude — an attitude for which his Rebbe, Rav Chaim Shmuelevitz, is best remembered — was actualized in a grand manner. Needless to say, this was by far the best-attended shul dinner. Prior to the dinner, the Rabbi had already made several trips to the hospital on his own to personally thank those involved in his recovery.

Honoring Winthrop and its dedicated staff was done exclusively because it was Rabbi Kelemer's request and the right thing to do. Nonetheless, there were some additional benefits from the affair. For Winthrop, there was a boon in the new awareness in the Jewish community (very well represented in that region of Nassau County) that the hospital was recognized as a top-flight medical center, just as competent as its New York City Ivy League colleagues.

An integral component of a patient's recovery is visitation by friends and relatives. This is eminently more doable in a Long Island hospital with ample parking, over a highly vaunted Manhattan alternative that can be reached only via snarled traffic, king's ransom parking, trains, subways and taxis.

There were also unintended dividends for the Young Israel community. Because of the dignified way the community acknowledged the hospital employees, when a religious Jew is treated at Winthrop, the administration sees to it that they are afforded the most gracious care. Furthermore, when Rabbi Kelemer suffered his stroke four years later, it was in the midst of the COVID-19 pandemic. The policies of virtually every hospital were non-negotiable at that time, but once again, for Rabbi Kelemer and his family, the hospital displayed remarkable tolerance.

CHAPTER NINE

His Busiest and Most Stressful Day

The willingness to go way beyond the call of duty was key to Rabbi Kelemer's astounding impact in both Brookline and West Hempstead. Word traveled fast that this was a community leader committed to going to extraordinary lengths to extend himself for the benefit of anyone who needed his assistance or guidance — although, as Rabbi Glanz noted, it wasn't necessary to be a member of his community to benefit from Rabbi Kelemer's eagerness to help.

Seventeen years ago, my grandmother passed away after a long bout with Alzheimer's.[8] It was the first time my siblings and I had lost a grandparent, and it was very difficult. After

8. Reported by Rabbi Daniel Glanz.

the levayah (funeral) my father asked me to take my brothers and sister in my car and drive in the back of the line of cars headed to the cemetery to ensure that no one got lost. As we were on our way the car suddenly filled up with smoke and I was forced to pull over onto the shoulder of the highway. Since we were the last car in line, no one noticed what had happened to us. Back in those days not everyone had a cell phone, which was unfortunately our situation.

After about fifty minutes had passed I had all but given up on trying to wave down cars and was thinking how this whole situation must have ruined the funeral and had my parents worried sick. Suddenly, a Rabbi pulled over to the side of the road. My little sister was on the verge of tears and he immediately took over the show. He calmed all of us down and, with a calm and warm smile, told us that he wouldn't leave our side until all had been settled. Since I did not know the name of the cemetery, he spent the next twenty minutes calling every cemetery in the area until he found the right one and left a message for my parents that everything was all right. He then waited with us for another forty-five minutes until the tow truck arrived, and he then loaded us into his car and followed the tow truck to the nearest service station.

After arriving I went over to him and thanked him profusely for all of his help. He told me that he had spoken with my parents and told them where we were and that they would be there shortly. However, as much as I tried to convince him that all was under control and that he could leave, he refused. He told me that he would not leave us until my parents had arrived. So we sat in his car and schmoozed for a good hour until my parents finally arrived.

Before this encounter I had never heard of Rabbi Kelemer, but I was blown away at his unbelievable willingness to provide a chesed for someone he did not know and how he performed the mitzvah beyond its completion.

Perhaps the most staggering part of the story is that Rabbi Kelemer is a very busy man who could hardly afford to give more than two hours to a complete stranger on a normal day. But as I found out later, this was not a normal day for Rav Kelemer. He was actually on his way to court to help someone in his community with a very serious issue. I later found out that it was actually the busiest and most stressful day of his career up until that point, and he managed to rearrange his impossible schedule and put the whole thing on hold for us, complete strangers!

Rabbi Kelemer's commitment might require him to drive across the country, endure all sorts of difficult weather, go for days with little or no sleep and overcome enormous obstacles, but it didn't matter. He would do all he could to make himself available. Once he began working to help someone with whatever their needs were, he was absolutely committed to getting the job done, regardless of the difficulty or scope of the task.

You Are a Physician, Aren't You?

THIS QUALITY OF *mesirus nefesh* (self-sacrifice) drew Jews from near and far to the West Hempstead community. The conduct had nothing to do with membership; it was simply the Rabbi's internal, ethical fabric.

Before my wife and I moved to West Hempstead, we were considering several different communities in the greater New York area. My wife had attended the bris milah of a friend's baby in West Hempstead. I could not attend because I was on call as a resident physician in a hospital in the Bronx.

When my wife came back from the bris, she could not stop talking about the wonderful Rabbi and how beautifully he spoke during the seudah at the bris. She had never heard anyone speak like that before. She told me that I would not believe what a wonderful Rabbi the community of West Hempstead had. I hadn't heard the drashah myself, but since she was so very impressed, it served as one of the contributing factors that led us to choose West Hempstead as a community to settle into.

When we finally moved in, we met Rabbi Kelemer briefly when he came over to introduce himself, welcome us to the community, and offered to kasher our kitchen late that night. The next day my wife was setting up her kitchen and she asked me to try and find the Rabbi and ask him a kashrut related question. It was 6:00 in the evening, so I wasn't optimistic that I would find him (I thought it was late; little did I know about Rabbi Kelemer's habit of serving the community until the early hours of the morning each day). I entered the shul and knocked on the door to his office. Rabbi Kelemer opened the door and saw me. Before I could say a word, he said, "You're a physician, aren't you?" I acknowledged it, and he said, "Please come in; you might be able to help me."

He explained that there was a conflict involving a husband and wife who were in the process of getting divorced in the community, and one took out an order of protection against the other, and then reported to the police that the other person had violated the order. As a result, this individual, who was an older man with a serious heart condition, was arrested and placed in a jail cell. As it turned out, at the time this individual was supposedly violating the order of protection, he happened to be meeting with Rabbi Kelemer.

When I came in, Rabbi Kelemer was busy making phone call after phone call, with the aim of trying to get this man out of prison, and if necessary to a hospital ward where he could be monitored for his heart condition. After making countless phone calls, he finally reached someone who was willing and able to give him the home phone number of the prison warden. Rabbi Kelemer called the warden at home, explained the situation, and tried to persuade him to release the prisoner — preferably to his home, but if not, then at least to a hospital prison ward. The warden refused.

Rabbi Kelemer continued to make what seemed like an endless series of phone calls, one leading to another, until at last he found someone who was able to give him the home phone number for the chief justice of the New York State Supreme Court. He called and woke the chief justice at his home at 11:30 at night and gently, but successfully, persuaded him to call the warden and order the release of the man who had been arrested. I don't know how long he had been working at this before I joined him, but I watched him for at least 5 hours of non-stop effort. I had never seen anything like it before. I came home and said to my wife, "You would not believe what kind of amazing Rabbi we have in this community!"

Not even a prison warden (or a chief justice) could stand in Rabbi Kelemer's way when he was determined to go to heroic lengths. Enlisting a young physician in this endeavor was simply part of the job. Mundane obstacles that present major challenges to most people (such as time, distance and sleep) were not barriers for him. He would drive across the country (he was unable like to fly) to visit a *choleh* or be *menachem avel*, or to be where he could benefit another human being in some way.

Even on a Seder Night

THOUGH SERVING HIS community 24/7 was a given for Rabbi Kelemer, Shabbos and Yom Tov meals were special for spending time with his own family. Those who knew him well tried to spare him from problems that would require him to sacrifice the few sacred hours he kept for his wife and children. Nonetheless, the call of duty he felt toward others could not be ignored, even as he sat at his table for the Pesach Seder.

> *It was Leil Seder. Our family was home for Yom Tov. We were well into Maggid, just before the meal, when we heard a knock on the door. It was too early for Eliyahu Hanavi. My wife answered the door as the rest of us continued around the table. To her surprise it was none other than Rabbi Kelemer. He didn't want to disturb and wouldn't come in. My wife went outside to speak with the Rav. He was looking*

The temperature was twenty degrees Fahrenheit, though the windchill factor made it closer to zero and the winds were howling. To the Rav, however, it didn't matter. What mattered to him was being present at a simchah associated with the community.

What was most outstanding was that after he spoke at the meal, he said his goodbyes and made his way out of the building, I later found out that the Rav then walked to Eitz Chaim for a bar mitzvah. Eitz Chaim is about a two-mile walk from where the aufruf was! This was Rabbi Kelemer. He always placed the needs and joy of others above his own.

A Very Productive Walk Home

EVERY FRIDAY NIGHT, Rabbi Kelemer oversaw a *tisch* for teenage boys, composed of learning and lively singing and rewarded with *divrei Torah* provided by Rabbi Kelemer, and carbohydrates (if the *tisch* was in the Kelemer home, provided by Rebbetzin Kelemer). One wintry Friday the Rabbi informed one of the young participants, Jordan Ginsberg, that he would not be able to attend the *tisch* Friday night, but it should continue as usual, albeit in two venues.

That Shabbos, Rav Novak — a disciple of Rav Shmuel Rozovsky from the Ponevezh Yeshiva and the *rosh kollel* of Da'as Yosef in Ashdod —

was visiting the community and was hosted by the Kelemers. Every *tisch* needs a Rebbe, and that week Rabbi Novak would be the "substitute Rebbe" in a *tisch* to be conducted at the Kelemer home. Therefore, after the boys had finished learning in the shul they were to head over to the Rabbi's nearby home for the *tisch* with the visiting *Rosh Kollel*.

Everything proceeded as planned, until the end of the *tisch* when, just as the boys were preparing to brave the rainstorm and make their way home, Rabbi Kelemer ran in and bounded up the stairs without saying a word.

The participants wished one another "Good Shabbos" and departed, but Jordan Ginsberg detected that even by Rabbi Kelemer's extraordinary standards (if ever there was an oxymoron...) something really newsworthy had just transpired, and sacrificing some sleep to learn about it would be a small price.

The next scene occurred in the kitchen where a drier version of the formerly soaked Rabbi Kelemer was now attired in Shabbos clothing. Rabbi Novak and Jordan entered tentatively and found the Rabbi alone, eating his Shabbos *seudah*. The Rabbi explained to his guest in Hebrew that there was a member of the shul whose mother was in Columbia Presbyterian Hospital in Upper Manhattan who had very complicated *she'eilos* that required extensive, on-the-spot involvement.

Rabbi Kelemer remained in the hospital as late as he possibly could to offer counsel and solace and then dashed outside to hail a cab. He instructed the driver where he desired to go, but there wasn't a prayer that he would get there before the onset of Shabbos. The routing was not helped by the very inclement conditions. If one had to pick all of the circumstances for a perfect Erev Shabbos nightmare, this situation was missing not a single component.

There was blinding rain, the driver was unfriendly and barely communicative in English, traffic was building up to stop and go at the good spots, and the sun was dipping like there was no tomorrow — certainly, no more today.

Rabbi Kelemer rode the cab as far as he possibly could before having to abandon ship — an apt analogy, considering the flooding over the roadways. Rabbi Kelemer thanked the driver for the adventure and then hurriedly stepped out into the deluge, sloshing eastward toward Long Island a *long* way away. Fortunately, the taxi managed to clock a few miles at the very end, which meant that an Olympic marathoner wearing the right gear and not battling a storm could probably break two hours to Hempstead at a sprinter's clip.

Well, what will it be? Rabbi Kelemer probably asked himself. *The Cross Island Parkway, the Grand Central, or the Southern State?*

There was a silver lining, insofar as traffic was *not* a consideration. But you would have to be Rabbi Kelemer to see the upside in that situation. Alas, Rabbi Kelemer was not thinking about that, or anything even remotely associated. It was now Shabbos and although his body was impossibly removed from shul, his head was already in a heavenly sphere. He had over three hours of splashing ahead of him and opted to invest the time in thoughts very distant from existential reality.

Meanwhile, Rabbi Novak and Jordan Ginsberg were slack jawed as they attempted to comprehend what Rabbi Kelemer had just undergone. The Rabbi, however, was unfazed (although he did seem to be nursing his soup). If Rabbi Kelemer had any regrets over his decision, he certainly didn't show it. As a matter of fact, in his typical jocular manner, he confided to Jordan that he'd had an exceptionally enjoyable walk.

Huh?

"*Gevaldig*," was the word that the Rabbi used. It was *gevaldig*, for along the way he comprehended the answer to a *kashah* of Rabbi Akiva Eiger on *Pesachim*!

For the uninitiated, a little background is indicated.

A question posed by Rabbi Akiva Eiger and

left unresolved remains the bar in the yeshivah world of the most inscrutable brilliance. If Rabbi Akiva Eiger, the genius of geniuses, could not answer a question, that means that it is beyond the realm of the most towering Torah sages. By way of analogy, an imponderable posed by Einstein in physics is not within the realm of entry-level, or even advanced, physics professors.

Let us, if we can, engage in antipodal conjecture as to what might be the best and the worst environments conducive to attempt to answer a Rabbi Akiva Eiger bombshell. So much erudition is required for the very attempt, that the best shot could probably be undertaken only in a *beis midrash* equipped with multitudinous volumes and graced by the presence of numerous scholars with whom to debate the logic and underpinnings of the matter.

Now, let us ponder where would be the *worst* place to propose a solution to the most ironclad of all questions. What immediately comes to mind is an environment bereft of *sefarim* and scholars.

The argument could be made that the bucolic countryside, absent of all distractions, might be concentration-friendly and stimulating to the brain. But this argument falls short when dealing with the caliber of a Rabbi Akiva Eiger question. Focus alone can not be adequate, for if the answer eluded the most accomplished and resolute scholar of his time, quietude itself will not bring about a resolution today.

But what we can agree upon is that a tumultuous, chaotic trudge through freezing rain as trucks gushed tidal waves at the banks of the roadway, and exhaust fumes choked the air, would be a challenging milieu to even remember one's name!

Alas, thus testified the man of truth. It was an enjoyable walk, indeed *gevaldig* — for among all the pandemonium of the Grand Central Parkway, where the noisy and odoriferous traffic roared like the surf, trudging and sloshing Rabbi Kelemer was a million miles away. His feet were plunging into rivulets, but his mind was prancing in paradise, joined by Abaye and Rava, Rav and Rav Ashi, Rabbi Akiva Eiger and the Pnei Yehoshua. Together with them, he was singularly focused upon plumbing the very depths of the Torah. On the banks of the Southern State Parkway, Rabbi Kelemer accomplished what only a select few in each generation can accomplish in a *beis midrash*: he resolved a question of Rabbi Akiva Eiger!

While we are attempting to highlight the improbability of such a feat, it should also be noted that *Pesachim* is one of the more challenging tractates of the Talmud. Only the truly learned have a full grasp of this *masechta*, and even among those few, rare are those who can comprehend the concepts without studying the words of the Talmud inside the text. Without the aid of a *Gemara*, even understanding the Gaon's question, let alone answering it — this is a non-starter for almost everyone.

For Rabbi Kelemer, even trudging home through a storm was an opportunity to learn Torah. Bad weather could never dissuade the Rabbi from being with those in need, especially if family members were unavailable.

In October 2012, my mom was in the hospital at Columbia Presbyterian, and Hurricane Sandy hit. I could not get into the city because of the severe weather, and I remember calling my mom and saying, "It's impossible to see you today." My mom said, "It's okay, Rabbi Kelemer is here with me." I immediately asked to speak to the Rabbi.

When the Rabbi got on the phone I asked, "Rabbi, how were you able to get into the city?"

He responded, "I happened to be in the neighborhood and am keeping your mother company singing Modzitz zemiros, so no need to worry."

Hurricane Sandy offered the Rabbi opportunities beyond singing *niggunim* to a woman stuck in the hospital. Since the fierce storm took out the power lines in West Hempstead, many people were unable to heat up food, since their stoves and ovens were no longer working. It was unclear how long this situation would last. Undaunted, Rabbi Kelemer stepped up to the plate, quite literally.

> *He stood outside West Hempstead High School during Hurricane Sandy in the pouring rain with the winds whipping up. He was outside kashering oven grates provided by Nassau County, available to be used by anyone who could kindle a fire and needed warm kosher food.*

Family Connection

RABBI KELEMER'S familiarity with his congregants was vast. He knew each of their names; how many were in their households and what they did.

> *I wanted to go back to Israel to study Tanach in greater depth, to support my teaching career. I was lucky to participate in Matan's Eshkolot program. Before I left, my sister became engaged, and we celebrated the engagement party a few days before I was scheduled to leave for Israel. Rabbi Kelemer came over to me at the party, asked how I was doing and what I was up to. I shared with him that I would be going to Israel for the year to continue my Torah learning. He*

inquired as to when I would be leaving and I told him, Sunday night. He wished me much hatzlachah in my learning and teaching, and expressed how excited he was for me. My parents had a family friend's wedding in Israel and we traveled to the airport together. As we were waiting in line to check our luggage, we suddenly saw Rabbi Kelemer at the airport coming straight toward us. It was 11:30 p.m.! He walked over to me and said, 'I just came to wish you a tzeitchem l'shalom — go in peace!' He sent me off with divrei brachah and Torah. To say that I felt like a million dollars is an understatement.

Rabbi Kelemer also knew where each of his congregants came from and where their parents and their antecedents came from. This information was culled from speaking and engaging with relatives. When grandparents came to West Hempstead for Shabbos, Rabbi Kelemer would open a dialogue with them, offering far more than just a courteous, "Good Shabbos."

He was genuinely interested in the guests that visited the community, and stories are legion of Rabbi Kelemer driving for hours to attend the funeral of a grandparent or even a more distant relative. All the information he gleaned was grist for the mill as to how to better relate to his congregants and understand their sensitivities — sometimes, even to save a life!

One young man from West Hempstead was engaged in a basketball game, during which he leaped for a rebound and suffered a very hard fall. His collapse was not the consequence of a foul or poor balance. Somewhere mid-leap he suffered a massive heart attack.

It was the kind of heart attack from which, as a rule, one does not awaken. Medically, he was finished. But that was when Rabbi Kelemer got on to the (figurative) court. He knew that this young man's grandmother, with whom he had spoken several times when she had visited, had an instrumental role in saving the life of the Belzer Rebbe in his flight to freedom from the Nazis.

Blond haired and blue eyed, she ran interference for the Rebbe, creating a diversion that enabled him to progress one more leg in his miraculous escape.

If medically there was no cure for a member of the Young Israel, that did not rule out other avenues. It was a long shot, but Rabbi Kelemer understood that you grasp at straws when a precious life is at stake. He immediately notified his brother-in-law in Jerusalem, the saintly Rabbi Chaim Walkin, who always acted as the Rabbi's go-to when he needed immediate assistance or cooperation from Israel's spiritual luminaries. Rabbi Walkin had the trust and the confidence of Torah's upper crust and had the ability to call upon them at any hour.

Here was Rabbi Kelemer's plan: The boy's grandmother as a little girl had risked her life to save the Belzer Rebbe; it was time to call in that favor. Rabbi Walkin reminded the Rebbe's court about the woman who had played a decisive role in saving the Rebbe by walking him across the plaza to a waiting car. And now, he notified them, her grandson's life was being decided in the Heavenly Assembly.

Instantaneously, the current Belzer Rebbe instructed a minyan to be assembled at the gravesite of his uncle, Rav Aharon of Belz. There, the *chassidim* stormed the gates of Heaven. The result, as far as mortals can fathom, was a medical miracle.

Those were the words of premier cardiologist Dr. Yossi Weisel, upon the sudden recovery of one whom they had already given up as being in the veritable foyer of the next world.

Therapeutic Sunshine

AFTER THE RABBI suffered a horrific hit and run accident, the West Hempstead community was in awe watching Rabbi Kelemer determined to get back to his pastoral duties. These were, as before, beyond the call of duty. Not content to give *divrei Torah* from the pulpit and teach classes, the Rabbi continued to visit folks in need of a kind word, company or medical advice. How did he endure all the strain and sacrifice to which he subjected himself in the course of doing all that he did? He was no longer young — at least not in body, although his mind and personality were always remarkably agile. He survived a devastating car accident that left him partially incapacitated. How did he have the strength to do it all?

A few weeks after the Rabbi came back to shul after the accident, I once asked him how he was mentally able to pull through all the severe pain and all of the struggles to get back on his feet and come back to shul and to the community. He told me that in his mind he went back to the shmuessen of his Rebbe'im at both the Telz and the Mir Yeshivot on inyanei emunah ubitachon — the topics of faith and belief — and that those messages helped him persevere.

The strength of these teachings did indeed carry him in the most difficult hours after being barreled over by a pickup truck. They were tested and reinforced as he met the needs of his flock, even more so when the COVID pandemic appeared.

The Talit family had been preparing for their son's bar mitzvah for years. Admittedly, the final months entailed the most intensive planning. But all the arranging and purchases were for naught when the pandemic hit. The Shabbos of the bar mitzvah, which had been planned as an affair of joy and accomplishment, with family and relatives joining from all over, ended up being just the nuclear family by themselves. There was no minyan, no reading from the Torah, and no one to listen to Joseph's well-prepared and memorized bar mitzvah speech.

Joseph's mom Michal took the decorations that she had purchased to enhance the synagogue hall and placed them throughout the house — a small vindication of the effort and expense. The family tried to make the most of the day they had looked forward to as Joseph's ascension into manhood.

On Shabbos afternoon, in the middle of a downpour registering somewhere between a downburst and a microburst, there was a knock on the door. This was totally inexplicable, as it was still at the early stage of the pandemic when social distancing was the norm, fear and confusion were all around, and no one went to a neighbor's door — certainly not when it meant braving weather that would have been challenging for a four-wheel drive vehicle.

The knock was so inexplicable that at first it was ignored: Either they were hearing things, or they were hearing what shouldn't be heard. But the knocking was persistent, albeit soft. Michal Talit went to the door and saw what she thought at first was an apparition. How could this possibly be? It was a pandemic, he was far from recuperated, and the weather was not fit for pedestrian traffic.

Yet there stood Rabbi Kelemer, all by himself, without an aid or escort. His black hat afforded him no protection from the rain, and he struggled to remain upright with his walker. Dumbstruck, Michal opened the door wide, unable to emit a single word in reaction to the most touching gesture she had experienced during her entire lifetime.

The Rabbi did all the talking. Despite the precipitation, Rabbi Kelemer's face erupted into a sunny crescent as he blessed, "Good Shabbos. I just wanted to wish you mazel tov and tell you all how proud we are of Joseph."

Forks of lightning electrified the cloud-laden sky, but this block in West Hempstead was bathed in therapeutic sunshine that only Rabbi Kelemer knew how to administer. When it came to people's feelings, he was the ultimate rainmaker.

Michal was so taken by the appearance of the Rabbi, that she began to tear and a lump lodged in her throat. She bade him farewell, then raced upstairs as she wanted to see from her window the Rabbi hobble away; an image that she would savor the rest of her life.

But, alas, he was gone; to where she will never know. Her unobstructed panoramic view from a corner house on the second floor showed no black hat, no man schlepping with a walker, just pouring rain, coming down furiously.

The Rabbi had vanished to his next angelic mission.

CHAPTER TEN

One Who Walks with Kings

Rabbi Kelemer's weak driving skills were the subject of many jokes. The reason the Rabbi refused to drive anything but a jalopy has been explained, but there was also an aspect intrinsic to the Rabbi's very persona. Independent of his gnawing conscience — "How can I drive a late-model car, when Ploni cannot afford to send his kids to summer camp?" — it also violated the Rabbi's nature to possess anything that was not basic and functional. This was not just because the purpose of a car is no more than to transport you from point A to point B, and the function of a sweater is to warm you, whether it is manufactured from polyester or cashmere. The Rabbi believed you paid a premium for purchasing premium.

Rabbi Kelemer wished to live the simplest lifestyle possible. Living in the relatively affluent Nassau County was not going to change this for him, but he felt one had to be constantly on guard. Once you own a designer raincoat, it must be paired with a costly Borsalino hat. Every purchase can make a barely perceptible yet insidious encroachment, and the Rabbi would have nothing of it. As an aside, driving a beat-up car also saved a fortune in bodywork that a luxury or late-model sedan would demand.

Even though good driving was not the Rabbi's strong suit, he was, oddly, a persona grata among the West Hempstead police force. In the course of their work, the forces in blue had encounters with him and were taken by his endearing charm. And whereas most cops believe that the terrified driver they pull over will reform, in the Rabbi's case they realized he was the exception and they did not hold this against him.

One time the Rebbetzin was pulled over in a nearby town for a driving violation, and when the cop inspected her driver's license and noted the last name, he asked her if she was related to the Rabbi. "He is my husband," she replied sheepishly.

The officer grinned and then uttered, in the curious patois of Coppese, "'Kay, go," and magnanimously waved her on.

Perhaps there was a redeeming aspect to the Rabbi's poor driving. Rabbi Kelemer was so kind, compassionate, wise and insightful that if he didn't have at least one glaring flaw he would be dismissed as too perfect. One cannot learn from and emulate one who is flawless.

Where Driving Fails, Try Walking

THAT RABBI KELEMER was a brilliant *talmid chacham* and an exemplary *baal chesed* was obvious to anyone who interacted with him. Many of his congregants thought of him as something more — a *malach*, perhaps? Yet when all was said and done, Rabbi Kelemer would insist, he was a man, no different from any other, just a member of the community. As such, he had a down to earth personality with an excellent sense of humor that endeared him to all and made him so pleasant to interact with.

His unparalleled greatness in Torah suffused his personality with a sweetness that made him beloved by everyone. To me, Rabbi Kelemer fit the description of the poet Rudyard Kipling, of someone who can "walk with kings" but not lose the "common touch."

Some of his congregants may not have fully appreciated the depths of his greatness in Torah, but they certainly appreciated his angelic character, soft spoken temperament, and incredible warmth. He was the embodiment of the Chazal that to be respected, one must perpetually honor others. Rabbi Kelemer always made you feel uplifted when you spoke with him. I can't tell you how many times I would go to him with a question or a thought in learning, and he would make it seem as if I had asked him an earth-shattering question or that I was somehow alluding to the myriad obscure sources that he had at his fingertips. He was deferential and so sincere that I really wondered if he believed that I was somehow greater than I actually was.

Rabbi Kelemer's sweetness included a wonderful sense of humor and a quick wit, which was apparent whenever he spoke at a *simchah* or even when he would give a *drashah* in shul. His brilliant mathematical mind enabled him to come up with amazing and lighthearted *gematria* in an instant, and apply them to the circumstances surrounding the family at any community *simchah*. He also knew how to use humor effectively when the situation called for him to prevent what might be an unfortunate situation from getting out of hand, without offending anyone. One shul member recalled vividly an amusing incident that took place at a *shalom zachar*.

As the Rabbi was about to speak, one of the attendees started kibbitzing every time the Rabbi tried to begin speaking. The Rabbi turned to this fellow and asked him what he was drinking. He answered, "Samuel Adams." Rabbi Kelemer responded swiftly, "Shmuel Adams, roshei teivos [an acronym] SHAAA." Everyone laughed and then the room fell totally silent.

Cracking a gentle joke is a great art. Greater still was Rabbi Kelemer's exquisite sensitivity to occasions that demanded words, and others that were best accompanied by silence.

Someone was once going through a really tough time in their lives and needed help. They went to Rabbi Kelemer to be comforted, to seek his advice, and just to have someone share their pain. They came to his house and sat down with him, and just began to cry. They were in so much pain that they couldn't utter anything; the words wouldn't come out. The person sat in silence sobbing, not being able to speak. Rabbi Kelemer, feeling their pain, with the most sensitive heart, also sat beside them in silence. This went on for what seemed to be an eternity but may have been a bit more than an hour, until the person seeking help felt they got what they needed, got up and left.

Rabbi Kelemer was a man who had innumerable responsibilities, none of which was neglected — and thus, every second of his was accounted for. It would have been perfectly understandable if after 15 or 20 minutes, he would have told the tearful person that he is sorry, and gently escorted him out. Instead, he just sat in silence for over an hour with this man, heart to heart. He did this not only because it was what this man needed, but also because due to Rabbi Kelemer's enormous capacity to empathize with others, he himself had shared some of that same pain.

My Lord, the Soul You Have Given Me Is Pure

THIS UNIQUE ABILITY to commiserate with any human being led him to work tirelessly to help people overcome their difficulties.

Rabbi Kelemer was the first person to help me realize what an abusive marriage I was in. I understand that many would have difficulty understanding this, but for others who have been in that situation, when you are immersed in such a horrendous cycle, and your self-esteem is non-existent, you truly don't realize the extent of the situation you are in. It was twelve years ago, yet I can clearly remember everything that happened in Rabbi Kelemer's inner office — those who have been there know what I am referring to.

He told me that every morning we say, "Elokai neshamah shenatata bee tehorah hee — My Lord, the soul that you have given me is pure," — and that I must recognize my self-

worth. To this day, as I write this, I am tearing up because I heard and felt the anguish that he felt over my situation pour out from him to me. He truly knew the depths of my despair. To see and hear him be so upset for me and my situation was my turning point. It is not a platitude or a cliché to say that Rabbi Kelemer saved my life; and in turn saved the neshamot of my children.

And in true Rabbi Kelemer fashion, his involvement did not stop with that one meeting. He referred this woman to a therapist, called frequently to check on how she was doing, and met with one of her sons one night at the Wing Wan restaurant for a snack and a schmooze. This child had not smiled or laughed in months, yet after 15 minutes he walked out grinning from ear to ear. How did Rabbi Kelemer do it?

I don't know what he said (I was waiting in the car), but I know that he made my son feel like he was worth a million dollars. It took another two years, but then Rabbi Kelemer performed another miracle for me, and I was given my get (Jewish divorce). He made me feel important and special at a time when I was at a complete low, through his display of true and sincere empathy. Every day since, when I say those words, "Elokai neshamah shenatata bee tehorah hee," I think of Rabbi Kelemer and thank him and Hashem for saving my holy neshamah.

Regardless of Affiliation or Affliction

THERE WERE NO LIMITS to Rabbi Kelemer's concern and responsiveness. He never shied away from making himself available to those who did not share his *hashkafah*, regardless of their religious affiliation. One Rabbi from a non-Orthodox synagogue recalled Rabbi Kelemer's helpful mentoring.

> *The Rabbi of my youth, from the time I was ten until I was eighteen, was Rabbi Yehuda Kelemer. Rabbi Kelemer was a strictly pious and traditional Orthodox Jew. Yet he always exhibited a warmth and open mindedness to everyone around him.*
>
> *One day in the 1980s, when I was a student at the Jewish Thelogical Seminary (JTS) I encountered him in the Seminary library. Why was he even there?*
>
> *He was doing research on the ketubah and came to the most highly regarded Jewish library in the New York area. I spoke with him about the education that I was receiving.*
>
> *Years later when I served a congregation on Long Island, Rabbi Kelemer was just a short drive from me. On more than one occasion, he would call to check on me. Occasionally, he would call to verify a piece of information or ask me about specific issues in the local community. He was warm, compassionate,*

and respectful — the same way I had known him as a young boy and also as a Rabbinical student.

Not only did Rabbi Kelemer give of his wisdom and concern to all, he also gave of his physical and spiritual energy, even in the most difficult circumstances. He was especially indefatigable in the fulfillment or celebration of a mitzvah. The remarkable commitment was contagious and impacted all those around him, even those in other congregations.

During the 2020 pandemic, Simchas Torah was unquestionably different. On what was many people's favorite holiday, suffused with singing and dancing together, this year the great energy and cheer was much harder to achieve than usual.

In order to stay safe in the face of the pandemic, the number of people allowed to enter the shul was limited, and all those who did enter the shul had to wear masks and stand by a chair that was set up far from those of others. Because of this, it was impossible to dance together in the way that celebrating the Torah most certainly deserves. Nevertheless, when the dancing started, people stood by their chairs singing, dancing, clapping and waving their arms to the rhythm, and the Torahs circled the bimah. However, it seemed to all a difficult task to truly mimic the fervor and great joy of the usual Simchas Torah celebrations.

Toward the final sets of hakafos, when even those who tried to dance were growing tired, in came Rabbi Kelemer with his walker through the Anshei Shalom double doors.

Once he strode in, with his walker before him, everything changed. He no doubt had already expended much energy dancing at the Young Israel, and then he undertook the walk to Anshei Shalom afterwards, despite his injuries — yet he was still able to radically restore the energy and passion back to the congregation.

Rabbi Kelemer was surely the oldest and least physically able person in the shul, yet he danced the hardest and with the most enthusiasm. Immediately upon walking in, he danced energetically by holding onto his walker, kicking his legs up in the air, jumping side to side, and singing with the biggest smile on his face. Those holding the Torahs, feeding off his energy, began circling Rabbi Kelemer instead of the bimah. The entire room was invigorated with the love of Torah, and fed off the great Rabbi's energy, and in no time, everyone was dancing as passionately as they ever had.

Rabbi Kelemer not only walked over to Anshei Shalom, but to all the other shuls in West Hempstead, a fatiguing task on its own.

He danced at each one with the same energy and passion, giving strength to all.

Another interesting aspect of Rabbi Kelemer's personality was his passion for music.

Years ago, I was at a community wedding and needed to find the Rabbi. I looked around the hall and then noticed that he was standing on the dance floor very close to the orchestra that was playing. I saw that he was paying very close attention to the music, with his eyes closed and a smile on his face. I approached him, and he turned to look at me, commenting on the superior ability of the musicians in this group and the beauty of their playing.

As Rabbi Kelemer was the son of a distinguished chazzan, I was not surprised that he took such an interest and had the ability to recognize excellence in music when he heard it. Still, given everything else he did, I was a little surprised that he took the time to notice.

I think, however, that for Rabbi Kelemer, music was more than simply something to enjoy; there was a spiritual component to it. Rabbi Kelemer liked to point out that according to the Zohar, the heichal of Moshiach is right next to the heichal of niggunim (Melachim II 3:15).

The Soundtrack of Our Lives

RABBI KELEMER'S EVERY action inspired his congregation to aim for higher spiritual accomplishment. While he was tireless in administering to each person's physical needs, he never failed to also administer to their souls. The most concrete way he did was through leading the davening on the holiest day of the year.

Michael Levine related that one Yom Kippur during *Mussaf* his grandfather unceremoniously collapsed and in short order was rushed to Mercy Hospital in Rockville Center.

When an elderly gentleman passes out there is naturally reason for concern. But being Yom Kippur, there was not much that the family and loved ones could do other than, appropriately, pray.

Rabbi Kelemer, naturally, did as everyone else in entreating our Father in Heaven to send a speedy recovery — and then characteristically, he did a tad more. Discreetly and inconspicuously, he slipped out of shul — and was immediately hit with a riptide of heat, as the temperature and the humidity were both in the high nineties.

Conceivably, there could be worse weather to walk along Sunrise Highway. Barely. For the uninitiated, there is something extraordinarily Orwellian in the name "Sunrise" Highway. A stretch of road winding its way through Long Island, any self-respecting stellar intergalactic twinkling celestial body would keep its distance from the least pedestrian-friendly road in America. Walking along this noisy, polluted artery, where vapor trails assault and envelop, and road detritus spews out like the spray from a hydrant wrenched open in the summertime, would have to be the least desirable place to be on Yom Kippur afternoon. And there was Rabbi Kelemer, hiking three scorching miles to the JV of medical centers, then another three similarly scorching miles back.

He did what he had to do, restoring cheer and hope, and then hustled back — along the malevolent crevasse of sundown highway — just in time to lead and inspire for *Ne'ilah* in Young Israel.

> *The Rabbi had a sweet, melodious voice. To hear it was a gateway straight to the heavens. In earlier years, he would daven Ne'ilah on Yom Kippur, and oh, how emotional that was. Other times as well. His soft voice making the brachah over wine, counting Sefirat Ha'omer in shul, lighting Chanukah candles, naming boys at brissim, reading the ketubah at weddings. That soft melodious voice is the very soundtrack that inspired our lives in West Hempstead.*

It was not enough for Rabbi Kelemer to move his congregation with his mellifluous voice. He was ceaselessly encouraging others in the community to dance and sing — especially in the honor of a new bride and groom.

Michael was part of a *chaburah* that met in the shul on Thursday nights to tackle Talmudic topics that require in-depth analysis. One Thursday night, just as the *chaburah* was getting settled, a youngish man, nicely attired and freshly shaved, barged in looking for something that wasn't clear.

"How can we help you?" everyone chorused at once.

"Uh, errr, umm, we are missing a minyan for *sheva brachos*. Might you be able to help us?"

The *chaburah* was pressed into dilemma mode. They had assembled for *talmud Torah*, and everyone was keenly aware of how paramount a priority that was. Furthermore, the *chaburah* met but once a week; it was now or never for the span of seven days.

"Who is the *chassan*?" one of the gentlemen asked?

"Well… I am," the groom responded, looking even more uneasy than before.

Upon closer scrutiny, it was manifestly obvious to the *chaburah* that the groom was not natively religious. This might have explained why the requisite number of men had not assembled, and why none other than the *chassan* himself had to go out hunting for a minyan.

Whether one was new to religious observance or not, it is not uncommon for a *sheva brachos* to be lacking the ninth or the tenth man, a deficiency that can usually be rectified with ease. It turns out that this *sheva brachos* was short no less than seven men — a whole *chaburah*'s worth — and no one had the temerity to disappoint the distressed *chassan*. Why, the whole purpose of *sheva brachos* was to instill and increase joy!

So, the *chaburah* relocated themselves out of the Young Israel and into a home around a table to join a meal that had not been on their night's agenda. Afterward, the men of the *chaburah* were unsure if they had indeed done the right thing, and brought their query to Rabbi Kelemer. The very Rabbi Kelemer that always made you feel that even if you didn't do the right thing, at least you intended to do the right thing. Rabbi Kelemer always saw the good in his fellow man, and imagined him to be of lofty character.

"You did the right thing," Rabbi Kelemer said, "for your hearts were in the right place. And undeniably, there should never be a situation where a *chassan* is in such a pickle. However, it might have been desirable had you at least learned five minutes. Certainly, the *chassan* would be understanding for such a minor delay and this way, not entirely uproot the *chaburah*. Alternatively, after attending the *sheva brachos*, resuming the *chaburah* would have been commendable." Gentler words could not have been spoken by anyone but the Rav who was respected by all Jews, near and far.

CHAPTER ELEVEN

Too Multifaceted

The attempt to compact Rabbi Kelemer's life into compact thematic chapters is doomed to fail, as his personality was so broad that it defied quantifying. As a tribute to the non-quantifiable aspect of the Rabbi, let us present some additional aspects of his impact and approach.

Rabbi Menachem Brick, a learned member of the Young Israel, was considering entering the Rabbinate. In preparation for this potential employment, Rabbi Kelemer proposed that they learn together *b'chavrusa* at night. "At night," of course, meant Rabbi Kelemer's understanding of that nocturnal phase.

Every night, the two met at 12:30 a.m., when they would analyze the *she'eilos* that had arisen that day, which Rabbi Kelemer had recorded in a little notebook. Rabbi Brick was sitting at the feet of the master, but Rabbi Kelemer always made his younger colleague feel he was an equally matched study partner and expressed his appreciation for Rabbi Brick's opinion on every subject.

At a certain point, Rabbi Brick lost his job. This was not public knowledge, but Rabbi Kelemer was aware. Somehow, Rabbi Kelemer always knew what was occurring with his congregants in real time. An opportunity to discuss this new situation presented itself as the two headed home from a *shalom zachar* on a frigid winter night.

Rabbi Kelemer not only steered the conversation in a productive way for Rabbi Brick, but also steered their perambulation to the doorstep of the Brick home. If there was anyone who should be escorted home, it was Rabbi Kelemer — and Rabbi Brick respectfully insisted on not entering his home until he had ushered the senior Rabbi home. Although all of this was taking place in weather cold enough to freeze lava, Rabbi Kelemer would not yield.

But when the Rabbi discerned the adverse effect the temperature was having on his former *chavrusa*, he relented and allowed Rabbi Brick to walk him home. That was fine, until they reached the Kelemers — and then Rabbi Kelemer turned on his heel and walked his colleague back to the Bricks' abode.

Independent of the snow all around, by now the reader has gotten the drift. Somehow, Rabbi Brick prevailed and walked the Rabbi home yet again. As soon as they reached Rabbi Kelemer's house, the elder Rabbi arranged for two of his sons to escort Rabbi Brick back to his family.

A Holy Society

RICHIE MILLER IS the head of the *chevrah kaddisha* in West Hempstead. This position afforded him frequent interaction with the Rabbi, as well as the ability to see him from a special vantage point.

As has already been noted, Rabbi Kelemer had the finely honed tact of knowing what to say and what not to say, as well as when to say it. As one can imagine, there is not much room for conversation when a loved one has just passed away. Indeed, the *Mishnah* teaches that we do not console a mourner when their dead relative is still lying before them.

And yet, many people have not learned or internalized this *Mishnah*. At this searingly difficult moment, conversation is not productive. Being present and listening is a source of solace and a balm.

Richie shared that he learned so much just by watching how Rabbi Kelemer conducted himself in these difficult situations. Standing on the side, the Rabbi seemed to be channeling strength to the mourners and words were not necessary. If a mourner wished to speak, there was no better listener.

Often, Richie would drive the Rabbi from the funeral home back to West Hempstead. During the entire ride, the Rabbi would retell positive anecdotes about the deceased and their family. Only someone who viewed every person as special could marshal so many nice things to say.

Rabbi Kelemer's consideration extended to everyone.

For many years, Jeremy Strauss served on the *chevrah kaddisha* of Queens. Jeremy is also a *mohel* and sometimes, tragically, both of these mitzvah avocations coincide. If a baby dies before he is given a *bris milah*, Jewish law requires that he be circumcised prior to burial.

And whereas a *bris milah* is always an occasion of celebration, a *bris* under these circumstances is poignant anguish. As the *mohel* holds the newborn in his arms, perhaps a part of him dies as well.

Jeremy Strauss was new to West Hempstead and, while he had performed this sacred mitzvah in Queens on several occasions, this would be the first time he was going to be doing so in his new community. It took a while until the hospital released the body and Jeremy did not actually walk out of the funeral home until 1:30 in the morning. As he headed to his car he saw something peculiar.

He knew why he was parked there so late at night – but what was that other car doing there, parked alongside his? On closer inspection, he noted that it was a run-down car with a man inside learning to the light of the overhead lamp. Of all times, and of all places!

The man in the driver's seat stepped out — and he was none other than Rabbi Kelemer. Because Jeremy had only recently moved into West Hempstead, the two of them had barely met. "*Shalom Aleichem*," the Rabbi greeted, extending his hand.

This is an odd venue to roll up the Welcome Wagon, Jeremy thought to himself. Then again, he was not yet familiar with Rabbi Kelemer's overarching sensitivity to others. The Rabbi understood how painful it must have been to circumcise a baby who was no longer living, and he wanted to be there to offer *chizuk* to the newcomer who had done such a valuable service to the newborn's soul, to the bereaved family and to the Rabbi's community.

Indeed, Rabbi Kelemer's sensitivity to others was the stuff of legends.

Sartorial Grandeur

ONE PASSOVER THE Strauss family was graced by the presence of the grandmother, Susan Rosenfeld, who was recuperating from back surgery. Because of her current medical condition, she would not have been able to walk to shul to recite *Yizkor* on the final day of Yom Tov.

The Strausses were not certain if the recitation of *Yizkor* necessitated a minyan, and Jeremy posed this question to the Rabbi on the first of the last days of Yom Tov. The Rabbi, in his soothing tone, assured Jeremy that God hears a sincere prayer recited anywhere.

On the final night of Yom Tov at 8:45, there was a knock on the Strausses' front door. There was Rabbi Kelemer; he wished to pay a call to Mrs. Rosenfeld, whom he barely knew. She was recovering from serious surgery and, from Rabbi Kelemer's perspective, inquiring as to how she was faring was surely indicated.

Not only was this visit an enormous boost for Mrs. Rosenfeld, but for the entire Strauss family... except one. Six-year-old Mordechai Strauss, clad in pajamas, was quite unenthused about seeing the local nobility that had just stepped through the door. Indeed, he died a thousand deaths from the embarrassment of the Rabbi seeing him on Yom Tov *not* wearing his finery, but... PJs!

Mordechai was surely not to blame. It was already 8:45 and, directly after the meal, he would be heading to bed. But still, in the mind of this first-grader, he had denigrated Yom Tov in the presence of his Rabbi, no less! Shamefaced and mortified, Mordechai could not even bring himself to look anyone in the eye.

At the conclusion of Yom Tov, the Strausses received a long email from Rabbi Kelemer extolling how Mordechai was the most Yom Tov-looking boy he had ever seen at that age. Indeed, he continued, it was sartorial excellence, and Mordechai's clean face and crisp PJs shouted "sanctity!"

"*Halevai*," the Rabbi wrote, "if only my grandchildren would look so *b'chavodik* and *Yom Tov'dik* on *chag*!" Rabbi Kelemer made six-year-old Mordechai Strauss, today a strapping lad at Yeshiva University, feel that he was on top of the world!

The Rabbi's ability to make others feel great was not only restricted to strangers. Jeremy Strauss, father of Mordechai-in-PJ fame, traveled to Kennedy International airport to pick up a relative. In an airport, as in any public place containing crowds so dense that people appear to be standing in queues just to walk across the terminal, it is difficult to recognize anyone in the sea of humanity.

But Jeremy Strauss did not have to be an observant Jew to spot Rabbi Kelemer hobbling with his walker, a wide smile on his face and a bouquet of flowers in his hand. The Rabbi was there to greet the Rebbetzin, who was returning at 5:30 in the morning from a very brief trip to Israel.

Always the Right Answer

RABBI JOSH GOLLER, a West Hempstead native, related that when one time when he came home from yeshivah to visit his parents, he attended the *shiur* the Rabbi delivered between *Minchah* and *Maariv*. The Rabbi, as he typically did, raised a question for the assembled to contemplate. The subject was *tirchah* on Shabbos, meaning that even if there wasn't a prohibition per se, one should avoid strenuous exertion on the Day of Rest.

One gentleman in the shul posed what Dr. Apfel labeled in a different chapter, "an off the wall question": "Shouldn't learning Torah on Shabbos be forbidden, as it is so strenuous on the brain?"

The very question caused some congregants to laugh uproariously, while others actually high-fived one another. Rabbi Kelemer, however, maintained a perfectly serious demeanor and responded, "For this very reason Rav Yaakov

Emden recommends that one utilize Shabbos to engage in *chazarah* — review of material that has already been mastered."

Once again, Rabbi Kelemer had marshaled his encyclopedic knowledge to turn an unlearned comment into an insightful suggestion, rescuing the dignity of the congregant in the process.

As was his nature, so was his speech. Rabbi Kelemer was a soft-spoken individual who never raised his voice. On one occasion, both Rabbi Kelemer and Rabbi Goller were attending a wedding in Long Island. As is so common these days, the music pounded at a shattering volume, which all but obviated the Rabbi's attempts to order a Diet Coke from the bar.[9]

Again, and again, the Rabbi placed his order, but the bartender, not schooled in lipreading, was at a loss as to what this gentleman wanted. Rabbi Goller was about to settle the problem with a loud baritone request, but the Rabbi made it clear that his colleague's assistance was not necessary.

Under the circumstances, Rabbi Goller began to wonder whether Rabbi Kelemer did indeed desire the beverage. Four or five attempts had gotten him no closer.

---

9. Because of its caffeine content, it was the Rabbi's go-to soda.

The answer was that the Rabbi did want the drink, but not at any cost. Under no circumstances did he wish the bartender to believe that the Rabbi was raising his voice at him.

Perceiving the Blessing

WHEN RABBI KELEMER was released from the hospital after his accident, he was sent to the Kessler Rehabilitation Center in New Jersey. It was announced in the Young Israel that in order to afford the Rabbi rest and tranquility to regain his strength and vigor, it would be best if visitors would refrain from traveling.

But Ari Hirsch could not stay away, and on one very rainy day, he drove down to Kessler. As it happened his visit was well-timed, and the Rebbetzin asked Ari to take over for a bit while she took a short break. It did not take Ari long to discover that Rabbi Kelemer was a veritable celebrity at the center. Young and old, patients and staff, all knew the Rabbi and afforded him much respect.

The Rebbetzin's absence afforded Ari Hirsch with the equivalent of a gold mine. He had Rabbi Kelemer all to himself for a solid 45 minutes. Far more important than the quality time, was the glimpse he got into the Rabbi's perspective — which took but a moment.

"Ari," declared the Rabbi, "what happened to me was a blessing!"

Hirsch adjusted his ears to make sure that he was hearing correctly. Rabbi Kelemer continued as if he was saying something no more surprising than the fact that the nose sits in the middle of the face. "Every week that I am here, another one of my children and their family comes to be with me for Shabbos. It is such a treat."

We can probably finish the thought, or at least how Ari perceived the comment. The Rabbi's devoted attention to the West Hempstead community left fully interacting with his family one more challenge that he overcame gracefully. But now that circumstances had presented this perk, the Rabbi chose to retroactively view the entire accident and the resulting requisite rehab as a pure blessing.

CHAPTER TWELVE

I Have Failed as a Rav, If Such a Question Could Be Asked

On a Thursday night in May 2001, a Jerusalem wedding morphed into an unprecedented tragedy. The dance floor, crammed with wedding guests clapping and dancing amid flashing disco lights and thumping music, suddenly collapsed, plunging hundreds of screaming celebrants into an abyss of concrete, sparks and dust.

Aside from the twenty-four killed, more than 300 people were seriously injured in the deadliest building collapse in Israel's history, all of it captured in dreadful wedding video broadcast all over the world.

The catastrophe, authenticated by the appalling film clip, was on everybody's lips that Friday and Shabbos. One congregant approached the Rabbi and asked if they should feel bad over the death of the irreligious Jews at the Jerusalem wedding. The questioner did not get an immediate answer.

That Shabbos the Rabbi visited every single minyan in the Young Israel. Generally, he would rotate between *minyanim* so that every few weeks, he would address each minyan; but not on that particular Shabbos. To each and every minyan, he repeated the question that was posed to him — and then said, "I have failed as a Rav, if such a question could be asked."

No Such Thing as Too Small

THE RESPECT AND love that the Rabbi felt for every person was legendary. Less well known were the small gestures that endeared him to so many — precisely because they reflected his caring in the most unassuming fashion. Each day, he greeted every congregant he met with warmth and care, taking time to find out what was on their minds at the moment.

Occasionally, I would stay after davening for a few extra minutes and daven a bit slower. I remember the first time I did this, I heard the sweet voice of our Rav taking time out of his jam-packed schedule to walk around to every individual in shul and wish a warm "Good morning!" When he encountered a member of the kehillah who was still davening, he would never just skip them. In the eyes of Rabbi Kelemer, every Jew was important and therefore he would always, without fail, say to the individual, "Please don't be mafsik... good morning." This seems so simple and small, but the truth is that for Rabbi Kelemer, when it came to being sensitive and genuinely concerned about others, there simply was no such thing as too small.

I remember that after davening, I would often see members of the kehillah flock towards him with she'eilos. Every time someone would come with a question Rabbi Kelemer would right away first ask the individual, "How are you doing? How is your family? How is..." Rabbi Kelemer took an interest in everyone, and he did so on a personal level.

When the time came for me to become a bar mitzvah, I began to meet the Rabbi regularly. One of the questions Rabbi Kelemer asked was, "What were some of your hobbies and interests from when you were younger?' I told the Rabbi that I collected pictures of Rabbanim. I remembered that earlier that day in yeshivah I had learned about Rav Yisroel Salanter, so I said that I had a picture of Rav Yisrael Salanter. Here's the thing: There are no pictures of Rav Yisrael Salanter in existence, only a picture of his son — and Rabbi Kelemer knew this. With his incredible sensitivity and middos tovos, Rabbi Kelemer just smiled at me and, with great simchah and care in his eyes, said, "Wow, that is amazing!" He went on to speak about Rav Yisrael Salanter for a moment to spare me from any embarrassment.

Easing a young boy into his bar mitzvah despite little fibs was a gift of spirit the young boy never forgot, but older members of the community had heavier worries. Each one found the Rabbi available to meet their sorrows despite his busy schedule. A mother of a child with special needs recalled his support when she was both parent and child.

Right after my mother's stroke, which was clearly devastating and put her life in imminent danger, I found myself thousands of miles away in Israel. I wasn't sure what to do. I called Rav Kelemer, and when he answered, it was clear that he was on his way somewhere. I asked his opinion, and he told me that in his experience it was important for a daughter to have an opportunity to say goodbye to her mother. Crying, I told him how difficult it would be for me to leave my family for an extended period of time, as I have a son with special needs. Without hesitating and in a calm and reassuring tone, he told me that my family comes first, and that my mother would want me to do what was right for them, and that at this stage, she would not at least consciously hear what I said to her anyway. He let me cry and spent a great deal of time reassuring me of my ability to make the right decision, even though it was clear to me that he was busy and had many other things to attend to.

Signed, Senator John F. Kennedy

SMALL GESTURES AMOUNTED to big kindness in the world that shaped Rabbi Kelemer. The source of his careful attentiveness to others, he claimed, was his father.

When Rabbi Kelemer was a patient in the emergency room of a neighboring hospital, I met him there and saw that just as he was being made ready for discharge, he made certain to take down the name and contact information of every individual (nurse, doctor and technician) involved in his care. I asked him why he needed this information. He told me that it was in order to send them all gifts afterwards.

He said this was a custom he had learned from his father. His father had taught him to always express appreciation for everything anyone does for you. He told me the story of how his father had once been traveling across the country by train many years ago. He traveled "coach" and slept through the night in his coach seat. In the morning when it was time to daven, he looked for a relatively private place to do so. He encountered a wealthy young man who was traveling in a private cabin on board the train and asked if he could borrow his cabin for a short time to pray.

The young man was willing to let him use his cabin, and Rabbi Kelemer's father was able to daven. When he finished davening, he asked his kind host for his address to send a note of appreciation. Upon arriving home, he sent the kind young man a bottle of wine and a salami as a token of his appreciation. Later, he in turn received a thank you note signed by Senator John F. Kennedy."

Whether thanking hospital workers or showing boundless respect for fellow Rabbanim, Rabbi Kelemer was known for his attention to detail.

We had a few occasions over the years to discuss communal issues that affected West Hempstead as well as my community. Rabbi Kelemer talked to me as an equal and was very interested in my opinion, despite the fact that he was head and shoulders above me in leadership skills, wisdom, and knowledge of Shas and poskim. He made me feel comfortable to express a different opinion than his, about any given issue. During his funeral, different people remarked that he was similar to a malach Hashem Tzevakot. I think that the reason why Rabbi Kelemer was similar to an angel is that he truly treated everyone he encountered like an angel.

In a Desperate Situation, Others Were Gone

RABBI KELEMER'S COMPASSION for other people's pain was evident to anyone who approached him with a problem. He showed endless patience and persistence in an unforgettable fashion. One woman, whose sister was in an unfortunate situation with a husband who out of spite would not grant his wife a divorce, recalled his ceaseless efforts.

Many Rabbis were involved in my sister's pursuit of her get (Jewish divorce). It was only Rabbi Kelemer who stuck with us through the years of the ordeal. Rabbis would come in all ready and willing to help and promising results, but when they saw the hopelessness of the situation, they were gone. Rabbi Kelemer stayed fast, always thinking of new plans, always consoling us, always making us feel that there was hope and an answer.

Rabbi Kelemer rallied other Rabbis all over the world to help us and supported us with words of chizuk and encouragement every step of the way. The phone calls were mostly past midnight, but he always came through and called. Even when he had no answer for us, he gave us hope that he would keep trying. Just speaking with him was a nechamah (comfort) and gave us the strength to go on.

His concern did not end with compassionate care. He went on to put together a group of three Rabbis, who came up with a particular approach to try and resolve the situation. The Rabbis asked that there be no contact with the husband's family during this time so they could work on their own plan. In our anxiety we found it was too difficult sit idle and wait. When the three Rabbis and our family had a teleconference to discuss the progress and they heard of our interaction with the family, one of the Rabbis became understandably upset, and raised his voice in rebuke, asking why we did not follow their directives. It was very hurtful, but before we could respond, Rabbi Kelemer jumped in and immediately consoled us.

"Of course we understand that your emotions were running high, and of course it was natural and normal for you to reach out." He continued to explain that we should not worry because it would not make a difference and it did not harm our case.

I do not know if he really believed that, but I do know that it made us feel better. Once again, he was there and always was there to make you feel the best you could. He carried my entire family through a most difficult and challenging time in the most soft, sweet, calming and delicate way that only a malach and shaliach of Hashem could.

That gentle, calm voice could be used to comfort as well as encourage his own congregation. He even went so far as to speak about delicate interactions between the Young Israel community and the Conservative school in town. In one of his Shabbos talks aimed at awakening the conscience of his congregants, he shared his opinion and pain.

His talk was about basketball so it really piqued my interest. In essence, the Solomon Schechter High School (a high school under the auspices of the Conservative movement) wanted to join the Orthodox High School basketball league, but was denied because they are a Conservative school and they could have a "bad influence" on our kids. The Rabbi was quite upset about this, and his take was that perhaps "our" kids would have a positive influence on them.

What Do We Do Without Rabbi Kelemer?

THE LEITMOTIF OF Rabbi Kelemer's life was his outstanding sensitivity to others. He was especially armed in this realm because of his mastery of Torah and keen understanding of human nature. Earlier we wrote about how the Rabbi would attempt to empower others, whether concerning their involvement with the Jewish community or resolving their own particular halachic dilemmas.

Now, already through the lion's share of the book, let's engage in an exercise.

Rabbi Kelemer's great *rebbi*, Rav Chaim Shmuelevitz, explained (a tad more sharply in Yiddish), "A student is not one who knows what his *rebbi* said, but one who knows what his *rebbi would have* said."

Like everything else in this volume, what follows is a true story, but it lacks Rabbi Kelemer's direction. Can we fathom what he would have guided?

The Steiner children were giving their parents a run for their money that could not have been imagined decades earlier. The Steiners, fine, upright individuals with a religious commitment rather typical of Young Israel families, sent their children to the local day school, expecting them to conduct their religious lives similar to what they had experienced at home and had observed in their community.

But one after another, this is not what happened. Already from the beginning of high school, the kids were becoming more religious than their peers. And when they spent their gap year in Israel, what was originally diagnosed as "a little more religious" became what some termed "full-blown fanatical," as *shanah alef* morphed into *shanah bet* and *shanah bet* transmogrified into *shanah gimmel*, until the point that it was meaningless to refer to their yeshivah study in yearly increments. Each child had become a "lifer," and college and America were off the table.

What were the Steiners to do? They implemented a series of measures, but details they had agreed upon — even *signed* upon — were of no avail. Each child got bitten by the bug, rejecting the way that they had been raised for a lifestyle that was significantly to the right.

There was but one Steiner child left, an 11th grader, and her parents were watching Sarah like a hawk. A gap year in Israel was never even a consideration for her. They did not know what had gotten into their kids — they had even considered checking their *mezuzos*! One thing was sure, Sarah was going to be shielded from anyone and any place that could send her off the religious deep end.

Sarah was well aware of the special attention that she was receiving from her parents. One nuance, just one intonation that could be interpreted as a deviation from her home lifestyle, would ignite the ire and protestations of her parents. But, as the winter approached, the elephant in the room got up and took a walk.

Kindhearted Mrs. Steiner bought Sarah a stunningly beautiful super-insulated winter coat. And not just any puffer, but a brand-name Jocada Down Parka. The kind of coat that goes on sale for $799. Mrs. Steiner got it for a bargain, a giveaway price! It was still deep into triple-digits, but still less than half of its retail cost.

What high school student wouldn't give anything for such an exquisite coat, the height of haute couture? Well, Sarah for one. The coat was indeed high fashion, stylish, lightweight, always the perfect warmth, practical… and also fire-engine red!

Even yeshivah-sheltered Sarah understood that it was immodest to wear a coat that virtually had neon lights flashing and klaxons ringing. What was she to do? Although the Steiners did not live in West Hempstead, whomever Sarah consulted about her dilemma informed her that only Rabbi Kelemer would be able to properly guide her when the first coat-wearing day of November arrived.

Despite extensive research, we have never learned what Rabbi Kelemer advised. Rabbi Barry Nathan, who brought the question to Rabbi Kelemer, passed away. Mrs. Linda Nathan remembers the question and the dilemma, but she was never apprised of the response.

After reading a book about the insights and methodology of Rabbi Yehuda Kelemer, can we divine what would he have advised? Obviously, it would be presumptuous and audacious to assume that we have the ability to render a decision as he would have — not to mention that we lack the scholarship, sensitivity and experience that he possessed in such copious amounts.

And yet, we, the unqualified, would probably reason that since Mrs. Steiner bought the expensive gift out of love for her daughter, and would be hurt (independent of the religious undertones of the decision) if Sarah were to shun the gift, this should be a factor in permitting the wearing of the coat. After all, the coat's immodesty is not in its cut or what it reveals. Perhaps nowadays, red is not the only color that draws the eye. Bright yellow, hot pink, and fluorescent orange also scream for attention.

Wouldn't making an issue over the color of the coat to such hypersensitive parents take a toll in other, more cardinal, realms of Jewish observance? One could argue that contradicting the express wishes of a parent violates the Biblical commandment to fear one's mother and father.

Even though modesty is a paramount concept, would this be on an equal footing with a Torah prohibition?

Rabbi Yitzchak Breitowitz has pointed out that many *poskim* maintain that honoring one's parents is not applicable in an instance where conduct would violate accepted norms of modesty, hence a definitive position cannot be adopted in the Steiner Catch-22. Furthermore, any assumption that honoring one's parents trumps modesty is a matter of halachic controversy beyond the pay scale of the garden variety reader to decide, based on common sense or emotion.

As unqualified as we are, we have still learned an approach from Rabbi Kelemer, as applicable regarding a red coat as it is regarding other aspects of family harmony, business dealings and interaction with others. We have seen repeatedly how Rabbi Kelemer would always weigh sensitivity and emotions with his keen sense of what a *psak* can or fail to achieve. As Rabbi J.J. Schacter labeled it, Rabbi Kelemer had the magic to make a *psak* work.

Regarding the Steiner dilemma, Rabbi Kelemer surely would have endeavored to find a peaceful and pleasant middle ground[10] to reconcile all the values at stake: the standards of modesty, as well as gratitude and appreciation for one's mother. He invested all of his energy into avoiding clashes, while at the same time remaining absolutely faithful to halachic imperatives.

We have become familiar with the Rabbi's approach, albeit are bereft of his ruling. We have yet to fulfill Rav Chaim Shmuelevitz's criterion of a student (partially because we are underqualified). Our predicament in light of Rabbi Kelemer's absence is soberly described in a Talmudic anecdote (*Berachos* 42b).

When the disciples of Rav returned from their master's funeral they sat down to eat along the Danck River. A question regarding *bentching* arose, which they could not resolve, and thus ripped their garments in mourning once again

10. Maybe (and pure conjecture) he would have suggested that Sarah tell her mother that she adores the gift, but would not enjoy wearing it knowing that it would engender envy among her classmates. She would appreciate if only she could acquire the exact same coat in a more neutral, less-envy-inducing color (like tan).

Since only the red coat was on sale it could not be exchanged for a different color, but Sarah could fib that she has a friend who knows someone at Bloomingdale's who would allow her to make the exchange. It would then be up to Sarah to clandestinely come up with the difference in price to effect the exchange. This is a reasonable cost to avoid immodesty and not antagonize her mother, who at heart wanted only for her good.

— for the pain of Rav's absence was rekindled afresh.

Rabbi Kelemer is gone, and every time we run into a quandary, his loss is acutely revived.

Can Flesh Respond to the Commands of the Soul?

MAYBE AFTER ONE keeps on giving, there is no more left to give. After a very difficult day engaging in his Rabbinic duties, four years after he was hit by a truck, Rabbi Kelemer returned home at 10:00 at night on December 10, 2020, and collapsed into his wife's arms. The Rabbi had been felled by a stroke and was rushed to Winthrop Hospital.[11]

Once again, the Rebbetzin headed out to Bubbe Mishket. The Rabbi had confided to his wife that he was named Yehuda after his great-great-grandmother Yehudis. The namesake had gone over to a distinguished Rabbinic guest to their Ukrainian village, the Apter Rav, whose coat was dragging in the mud, and lifted the coattails. The grateful guest turned around and blessed

11. The community rallied to generate merits for the Rabbi's recovery. Among the efforts was the commissioning of a *sefer Torah*, which was not completed in Rabbi Kelemer's lifetime. When the writing was concluded there was a beautiful and grand celebration to honor the *sefer Torah* that would be read from every Shabbos in the Young Israel.

her, "*Arichas yamim, arichas yamim* — may you be blessed with a long life!"

The Rebbetzin always interpreted this anecdote as a sign that the Rabbi would also be blessed with long days. Rochi Kelemer reported to her unconscious husband about her mission to Bubbe Mishket. The Rabbi was unable to speak but an enormous tear slid down his face as he perceptively shook his head from left to right. This time, he understood that it wouldn't work.

The effects of a stroke vary in severity and from person to person. Rabbi Kelemer's was of the gravest type, for he was knocked unconscious and did not emerge from his hospital bed. Remarkably, however, the day before his last, he snapped out of his coma and was fully on top of his game. For one day, it was as if nothing had happened. Of course, no one knew that that there would be only one day of lucidity before the onset of another stroke, which ultimately claimed his life.

Dr. Abe Peller is on staff at Winthrop Univeristy Hospital (now known as NYU Langone Hospital — Long Island) and was intimately involved with both of the Rabbi's ordeals there. He made himself extra available on the day that the Rabbi awoke. A picture was taken of Dr. Peller at Rabbi Kelemer's bedside and the Rabbi, face tucked in an oxygen mask, is clearly smiling and his eyes are aglow. In the foreground, the Rabbi is holding one thumb aloft, but his "thumbs up" gesture is different than the generic universal pose featured so often in Zoom meetings and selfies. That gesticulation was a tad too cool for the Rabbi. If one would scrutinize the shot a little closer, one would discern that what he was really displaying was a cross between the emoji image one receives in a WhatsApp message several times a day, and the *grubba* finger (thumb) dancing in concentric circles in the air as one comprehends a passage of the Talmud.

That was the Rabbi — a synthesis of the *beis midrash* that never left him, and his adaptation to make himself an effective contemporary teacher and leader.

Years earlier, one congregant (let's call him Yosef) had approached Rabbi Kelemer with a proposal. Yosef asserted that there was a special pleasure that a parent derives from buying a gift for their child. However, for those struggling with their utility bills and a host of other expenses, there was no change left over for this luxury. Accordingly, Yosef generously underwrote what he labeled a "toy drive." This seasonal campaign took place during Chanukah, a time when children would see their friends displaying new gifts, and would naturally feel left out if they received none.

The key to the toy drive was Rabbi Kelemer, who tactfully and discreetly distributed store gift cards to parents who were struggling financially. (If he were consulted as to which would be the preferred store, he would display his ignorance regarding this temporary world by commenting, for example, "I don't know if you should go with Amazon, as they ship, and you know that deliveries are not always reliable.") Sometimes there was money left over, which the Rabbi knew just how to allocate.

He knew the birthdays of the children of his *kehillah* and he would propose to the parents that they use a gift card to underwrite a birthday present. When the Rabbi emerged from his month-long coma at Chanukah time, he immediately fretted about the disadvantaged children that he normally served at that time of year. "Have they been looked after? Did they get their gifts?"

The Sages have taught that man's true character is revealed in three areas: his finances, his flask and his fury. When it comes to money matters, when he is "in his cups," and when he loses his temper, a man's rein on his natural impulses snaps and the opaque shield behind which he conceals his inner self becomes transparent and clear to all.

There is, however, one more state wherein man is stripped of his defenses: his infirmity. Can a fevered brain be made to respond to the commands of the soul? The answer, obviously, is yes

— when the soul has so saintly a master as Rabbi Yehuda Kelemer.

The "Student" Who Saw the Silver Lining

THE TITLE *TALMID CHACHAM* is awarded to one who has a mastery of Torah learning and is fluent in every aspect of the Talmud and *Shulchan Aruch*. This translates to "wise student," implying that no matter how erudite the scholar is, he still views himself as a student with much more to learn. Even at the very end, this was a very apt term for Rabbi Kelemer.

Rabbi Joshua Goller, Rabbi Kelemer's associate Rabbi, who also enjoyed overwhelming admiration from the Young Israel congregation, had the entire shul resting upon his broad shoulders. He called up the day that Rabbi Kelemer was extubated, and the senior Rabbi shared with his younger colleague what a "student" he still was.

Being in the hospital was an opportunity to learn from the employees — from the phlebotomists to the dieticians, to the medical students who joined the rounds, to the janitorial crew to the nursing staff, all of whom were engaged in one way or another in the convalescence of the patients. None of them were working for themselves but rather for the betterment of others. Therefore, the Rabbi concluded, "I have a lot to learn here. I have been sent to this *beis midrash* to observe how to better engage in and strengthen my commitment to *chesed*."

This was the *talmid chacham* aspect of the Rabbi. Who in this generation was a peer to Rabbi Kelemer in *chesed*? The one who secretly walked six hours in the heat on Yom Kippur to visit someone just admitted to the hospital, who kept company at midnight with a young man diagnosed with ASD, the Rabbi who at 1:30 in the morning was scouring the bars of Boston looking for an unidentified diabetic college student, the one who drove for over an hour to a hospital on a weekly basis to see if there were any patients who might appreciate a visit, the one who was able to spin a thoroughly botched *dvar Torah* into a brilliant insight and attribute all the erudition to the novice, the one who could feign laryngitis to gladden a *chassan*... This was the "student" who saw the silver lining, that God had placed him in the hospital to learn how to improve his *chesed*.

I Suppose You Did Not Hear the Rabbi

RABBI KELEMER, JUST extubated and still connected to numerous tubes and monitors, expressed what he normally would never talk about but simply execute. He could not wait until he would be able to visit other patients in the hospital. He could not move, but he was already plotting what his first moves would be. This is a familiar scene. Avraham Avinu was suffering from post-operative pain and on the day of his most intense agony, what anguished him most was his inability to be hospitable. When you are focused upon others, then life — no matter how it is dished — is a cornucopia of opportunities.

The Talmud explains that the verse in Proverbs, "The wise of heart will seize good deeds" (10:8) refers to Moshe. While the entire nation was collecting spoils from Egypt, Moshe was gathering the bones of Yosef to bring them to burial in the Land of Israel. It was a time of enormous opportunity, and Moshe, the one blessed with a wise heart, saw that the greatest prospect was to do for others and not concentrate upon himself.

Rabbi Goller pointed out that when *his* son was admitted to the hospital, he spent the night sleeping at his son's bedside. Rabbi Kelemer encouraged his colleague to take advantage of being in the hospital, especially at odd hours, to visit others and bring them cheer. Initially, Rabbi Goller was focused exclusively on his ailing son, until Rabbi Kelemer was able to help him to turn — indeed, sanctify — challenges into opportunities to benefit others.

While in the hospital, Rabbi Kelemer had another experience when a nurse attempted to draw blood for a test. True, it is challenging to locate just the right vein in a senior, but this nurse was unable to execute a hit in over a dozen tries. Those from Rabbi Kelemer's family who were at his bedside were well-attuned to their father's manner, and could tell how much pain he was in, but the nurse surely did not, for he was smiling and kept complimenting her at her perseverance and noble efforts. "You are such a wonderful, patient nurse!"

The reader will recall how many actions and reactions of the Rabbi were compared to the deeds of Rabbi Chaim Shmuelevitz, Rabbi Nochum Percowitz and Rabbi Shlomo Zalman Auerbach. In this instance, the script was taken directly from Rav Moshe Feinstein. Toward the end of Rav Moshe's life, he had to undergo a biopsy — a painful test that involves the insertion of a long needle deep into the body in order to remove a tissue sample. Prior to this procedure, Rav Moshe had endured without protest batteries of tests that were not only painful but degrading as well. This particular test, however, Rav Moshe found too agonizing to bear, and asked the medical technician to remove the needle.

Over his patient's protests, the technician continued to jab deeper, assuring Rav Moshe that the procedure would take only a few more seconds. It is not uncommon for hospital staff to become inured to the patients' complaints, particularly when a test performed routinely is known to be painful but is essential for diagnostic purposes.

"I suppose you didn't hear the Rabbi," Rav Moshe's son-in-law intervened and physically withdrew the technician's hand. Surprised, but unwilling to counter the authoritative voice of Rabbi Moshe Tendler, the technician packed his equipment and prepared to leave. Just then, Rav Moshe's attendant informed the medical technician that the Rabbi wished to speak to him.

The technician was certain that the Rabbi intended to upbraid him personally for having caused him discomfort and for attempting to continue against his will. Rav Moshe, however, had something else in mind. Through an interpreter, he conveyed to the young man his gratitude for the service rendered. "I understand that you were only doing your job and trying your hardest."

What's Mine Is Really Hers

THE ALMIGHTY HAD graced the Kelemer family with one last day of the Rabbi fully coherent. That night he suffered his final stroke and the summons arrived from the Yeshivah Above. Everyone below was left bereft.

On Sunday, January 10, 2021, in the midst of the pandemic, Rabbi Kelemer was brought back to his beloved Young Israel of West Hempstead for the final time.

When the Rabbi would speak, he would always look down. He was not scanning notes, for he always spoke extemporaneously, other than regarding the names of visiting relatives, for he loved to welcome them by name. Now, the celestial beings were surely looking down and shedding tears.

Because of COVID-19 restrictions, only a limited number were allowed inside the shul while over 20,000 people watched the service though Zoom. Undoubtedly, had it been a funeral for *anyone else*, despite the plague or any other present danger, Rabbi Kelemer would have attended. Among the honored guests allowed inside were the Rabbi's *mechutanim*, Rav Shmuel Kamenetsky, *Rosh Yeshivah* of the Yeshiva Gedolah of Philadelphia, and Rav Elya Chaim Swerdloff, *Rosh Yeshivah* of the Yeshiva Gedola of Paterson. The eulogizers were united in extolling the Rabbi's mastery of Torah and halachah, his compassion, sensitivity, and ability to listen. Most of his kindness, it was declared, will never be revealed, for that was the way he wished.

Rabbi Elya Chaim Swerdloff, in his stirring eulogy, analyzed the two expressions used for shepherds. The standard shepherd uses his staff to drive any wandering sheep back to the flock. The *ro'eh bashoshanim*, however, is not equipped with staff, but instead clutches a bouquet of roses. This shepherd, like the proverbial educator who uses honey, guides his entire flock with the fragrance of flowers.

Because Rabbi Kelemer's personality and methodology were so pleasant and appealing, he never employed a harsh word. Roses encourage amenability; a staff foists obedience.

The eulogizers conferred special acknowledgement to the behind-the-scenes support and encouragement of the Rebbetzin, whom the Rabbi had often referenced with the words of Rabbi Akiva, "*sheli shelah*" — what's mine is really hers, as he acknowledged that it was his Rebbetzin's sacrifice that allowed him to tend to others.

Indeed, the entire Kelemer family shared their father with the community and did not demand the extra attention that was due them. His children would have been pleased to welcome Friday night at the same hour as everyone else, but it would be several hungry hours before their father returned home from wishing the widows and the infirm a "Good Shabbos."

In his eulogy, Rabbi Yosef Kelemer, Rabbi Yehuda Kelemer's son, took note of the fact that one of technology's most utilized buttons is "delete." One is never more than a keystroke away from the opportunity to delete and rewrite. Yet Rabbi Yehuda Kelemer's life did not need such a convenience. He did not live his life in regret over how he should have held his tongue or extended himself further. He invested all his intellect, magnanimous heart, and finely honed sensitivity into getting it right the first time.

Going a Little Higher

YOSEF ALSO RELATED that the Chofetz Chaim lived in the remote village of Radin, off the beaten path, uniquely isolated from any urban center. Accordingly, many prominent Jews wanted the Chofetz Chaim relocated to a major urban community on the crossroads of civilization so that greater numbers could take advantage of his saintly scholarship. Yet mission after mission failed. One delegation went so far as to descend upon Radin in the as-yet-unseen contraption known as an automobile. Being beamed up to the Starship *Enterprise* would have been no less revolutionary in Radin in the late 1920s.

The villagers of Radin, rather than being amazed by the wonder that had just appeared in their townlet, dismissed it with the same disregard they had afforded all the other committees that had come to displace their master. When the delegation emerged from the Chofetz Chaim's hovel, they found their car had been physically lifted and deposited in a field. The message was clear: the Chofetz Chaim, with all his reluctant fame, was inextricably bound to Radin. The nondescript town would have remained anonymous if not for the Chofetz Chaim, and likewise, the Chofetz Chaim would not be who he was without Radin.

Concluded Yosef Kelemer, to an audience whose eyes were bathed in tears, Rabbi Kelemer not only graced West Hempstead for thirty-eight years, but he — the most unlikely and overqualified of Rabbinic candidates to serve in a Young Israel synagogue in suburbia — could not have become the unparalleled spiritual leader that he was without West Hempstead.

Rabbi Shmuel Dovid Kelemer invoked in his eulogy the story of *im lo l'maalah mizeh* for which this book is titled. Whatever complimentary attribute you could ascribe to a holy man, the members of the Young Israel believed that *their* Rabbi was yet higher.

It should be noted that West Hempstead is a commuter town comprised of intelligent, college-educated professionals. And just as every community has no shortage of cynics who make it onto the shul board just to ensure that the Rabbi has a dynamic relationship with his cardiologist, West Hempstead could have and might have been the same — had it not been for the Rabbi's nature and erudition which were above — indeed, higher — than critique.

Once word of the Rabbi's passing spread, there arose a granite-like resolve that everyone, just like their Rabbi, could reach a little bit higher. In accord with the chassidic maxim, "There is nothing more complete than a broken heart," there was overwhelming commitment to avoid being petty, unforgiving, and egotistic. On the contrary, *oib nisht noch hecher* — if not higher — as much as possible like Rabbi Kelemer. The community that had been blessed with Rabbi Yehuda Kelemer for nearly four decades owed him a firmer resolve to avoid the need to "delete." There was a commitment to extend themselves for newcomers, to be concerned about the welfare of neighbors' children, and to express gratitude wherever appropriate, whether to stranger or family.

Not in the First Row

MANY PEOPLE interviewed for this book employed the term "angel" to describe their Rabbi. Not wishing to engage in often-spurned hagiography (like the *misnaged* who was skeptical about the Rebbe, and the naive *chassidim* who adored him) this writer attempted to avoid utilizing this appellation to describe the Rabbi. And yet, more than anything, Rabbi Kelemer was a teacher, about which the Talmud proclaims, "If your teacher resembles an angel of the Lord of Hosts, then seek Torah from him" (*Moed Kattan* 17a).

This is a remarkable statement, considering that we haven't a clue as to what an angel looks like or how it conducts itself. One would imagine that clearer guidance would be indicated for something as essential as selecting a teacher.

Rabbi Leib Bakst, *zt"l*, explained that we know very little about angels, other than that they can do but *one* mission. In this regard, Rabbi Kelemer was truly angelic. His singular mission was to do the will of the Lord and live for others, whatever this entailed. Therefore, every encounter with him made a person feel more special, aspiring to reach higher. After speaking to the Rabbi, people walked away wishing to speak more kindly to their spouse, desiring to commit to greater Torah learning, be better focused on others and the community, and mindful not to employ disparaging remarks about those who were less religiously observant — even if it meant employing a virtual microscope to see the good in others. That was his single, solitary mission, to which he devoted his every day.

There was discussion as to where the Rabbi should be buried. There was discussion, but it was manifestly clear what he would have wanted. As in life, he wished to be together in the *beis hachaim* with his congregants in the Young

Israel section of New Montefiore Cemetery. The shul felt that it was only fitting that he be buried in the first row, but his Rebbetzin objected.

Rabbi Kelemer in the front row? This is exactly what he shunned! Every morning after davening, congregants would approach with their *she'eilos,* and then the Rabbi would circulate among *all* the rows, blessing everyone and wishing them a good day.

The front row? That would be appropriate for someone who sought honor; the Rabbi eschewed it. And as the Sages teach, whoever flees from honor, honor runs after them. Who in Long Island has not heard of Rabbi Kelemer?

Rabbi Yehuda Kelemer, *zt"l,* is remembered by all with appreciation, love and a resolve to honor their Rabbi by improving themselves. When the small, COVID-era funeral party arrived at the Young Israel section of the cemetery, it was striking how Rabbi Kelemer's words could be found on so many of his congregants' family tombstones. Soon, the singularity of his angelic mission, which had been hewn into the hearts of his community, would be engraved in stone.

He had traveled far. From Miami to Los Angeles, to New York to Detroit to Cleveland to Jerusalem to Montreux to Middle Village to Brookline to West Hempstead, to Heaven. If not higher.

Glossary

The following glossary provides a partial explanation of some of the foreign words and phrases used in this book. The spelling, tense, and explanations reflect the way the word is used in *If Not Higher*. Often, there are alternate spellings and meanings for the words. Foreign words and phrases that are immediately followed by a translation in the text are not included in this section.

ACHARONIM: lit. the last ones; the Torah scholars of the past five hundred years.

ADAM GADOL: lit. a great person; a spiritual giant.

AUFRUF: (Yid.) the custom of calling the bridegroom up to the Torah on the Sabbath preceding his wedding.

AMUD: half of a folio of Talmud.

ANIVUS: humility.

ARICHAS YAMIM: to live a long and fulfilling life.

AVEILUS: a state of mourning.

AVRAHAM AVINU: Abraham our forefather.

B'CHAVRUSA: with a learning partner.

BAAL MUSSAR: a master of ethics.

BAAL SIMCHAH: the host of a celebration.

BAALEBATTIM: (Yid.) laymen; one who has an occupation other than full-time Torah study or education.

BAR/BAS MITZVAH: the age of a child reaching maturity: 13 for a boy and 12 for a girl, a cause for celebration.

BARUCH HASHEM: thank God.

BASHAMAYIM: in the heavens.

BAVA METZIA: a tractate in the Talmud.

BEIN HASHMASHOT: lit. between the suns; twilight.

BEIS MIDRASH: a yeshivah study hall.

BERACHOS: a tractate in the Talmud.

BIKUR CHOLIM: lit. visiting the sick.

BIMAH: a podium for the Torah reading in the synagogue.

BNEI YESHIVAH: lit. sons of yeshivah; students.

BRACHAH: a blessing.

CHAMETZ: lit. leaven; food that cannot be eaten on Passover.

CHASSAN: a bridegroom.

CHASSID, CHASSIDIM: the follower(s) of the teachings of the Baal Shem Tov.

CHAZAL: 1. an acronym for our Sages, of blessed memory; 2. a statement by the Sages.

CHAZAN: a cantor; the leader of public worship.

CHESED: deeds of loving kindness.

CHEVRAH: society.

CHIDDUSH: a novel insight in Torah interpretation.

CHIDON HATANACH: a Bible contest.

CHOLEH, CHOLIM: one(s) who is (are) sick.

CHUMASHIM (pl.): the five books comprising the Torah.

CHUPPAH: a wedding canopy; the marriage service.

DAF GEMARA: a folio of the Talmud.

DARKEI SHALOM: paths of peace.

DRASHAH, DRASHOS: a Torah sermon(s).

EREV SHABBOS: the Sabbath eve.

GABBAI, GABBA'IM: the warden(s) of the synagogue.

GADOL: a great Torah personality.

GADOL B'YISRAEL: pious scholar of renown.

GAON, GE'ONIM: genius(es) in Torah scholarship.

GEDOLEI HADOR: lit. great ones of the generation.

GEMARA: the commentary on the *Mishnah*, which together comprise the Talmud; a volume of the Talmud.

GEMATRIA: the numerical equivalencies of the Hebrew alphabet.

GET: a divorce, the divorce document.

GEVALDIG: (Yid.) wonderful.

GEVUL: a border.

GRUBBE FINGER: (Yid.) a thick finger, thumb.

HAKAFOS: lit. encircling with the Torah scrolls on the holiday of *Simchas Torah*.

HALACHAH: Jewish law.

HAMOTZI: the blessing on bread.

HASHKAFAH, HASHKAFOS: outlook(s).

HASHKAMAH MINYAN: early rising prayer quorum.

HATZLACHAH: success.

INYANEI EMUNAH UBITACHON: subjects pertaining to one's belief and trust in God.

KABBALAS SHABBOS: the prayers said to usher in the Shabbos queen on Friday night.

KALLAH: a bride.

KASHAH: (Yid.) a question.

KASHER: to render a utensil kosher; such as by boiling it or burning it.

KAVOD ACHARON: lit. final honor or last respects, such as putting up a tombstone.

KAVOD HABRIOS: giving respect to God's creations.

KAVOD HAMET/HAMEIS: honor due to the deceased.

KAVOD HATZIBBUR: honor/deference for the congregation.

KEVURAH: a burial.

KIDDUSH: lit. sanctification 1. a ceremony over a cup of wine ushering in the Sabbath or holiday 2. a celebration usually in a synagogue on a Sabbath morning for the birth of a girl.

KINUSS BNEI HAYESHIVAH: an assembly of yeshivah students.

KOLLEL: an institution or organization of full time Torah learning for married men

KOLLEL AVREICH: a man who learns in a *kollel*.

L'MAALAH MIN HAZMAN: transcending time.

LEHRNEN: (Yid.) learning.

LEIL SEDER: Passover Seder night.

LEIL SHABBOS: Friday night.

LEVAYAH: a funeral.

LEVUSH: clothing.

MAARIV: the evening prayer.

MACHLOKES: discord and strife.

MACHMIR: stringent in matters of Jewish law.

MAGGID (of the Seder): the section in the Haggadah (the text used at the Passover Seder) that retells the history of our redemption from Egypt.

MALACH HASHEM TZEVAKOS: an angel of the Lord of Hosts.

MARA D'ASRA: the Rabbinic authority of a town/congregation.

MAREI MEKOMOS: a list of sources.

MASKILIM: Jews who had forsaken their Judaism due to the "Enlightenment" movement.

MECHILAH: pardon, forgiveness.

MECHUTAN/MECHUTANIM: the parent(s) of one's son-in-law or daughter-in-law.

MEKUBAL: a kabbalist; a Jew who studies the esoteric, mystical text known as *Kabbalah*.

MENACHEM AVEL: visiting a mourner.

MESADER KIDDUSHIN: the one who officiates at a wedding.

MESHULACH: an itinerant fund raiser for a charitable institution.

MESIRUS NEFESH: self-sacrifice.

MIDDOS TOVOS: good character traits.

MINCHAH: the afternoon prayer.

MINYAN: a prayer quorum of ten men.

MOTZAEI SHABBOS: Saturday night, after the conclusion of the Sabbath.

MUSSAR: 1. a school of thought emphasizing ethics 2. moral teachings, 3. ethical lecture.

NESHAMAH: the soul.

NIGGUN, NIGGUNIM: tune(s) or melody/ies.

PARASHAH: weekly Torah portion read in the synagogue.

PARASHAS VAYISHLACH: the Torah portion of Vayishlach.

PASKEN: a ruling; a halachic decision.

PESACH: Passover.

PESACHIM (GEMARA): a difficult Talmudic tractate discussing the laws of Passover.

PISKEI HALACHAH: halachic decisions.

PLONI: a person unknown and unnamed; compare to "John Doe".

POSEK: a rabbinical authority.

PSAK: a halachic decision.

PSHAT: the plain meaning of the text.

RABBANIM: rabbis.

RAV HAMACHSHIR: the rabbi awarding a kosher certificate.

REBBE: the rabbi of a chassidic sect.

REBBI, REBBE'IM: a rabbi(s) who teaches students in a yeshivah.

RIBBONO SHEL OLAM: the Almighty Creator of the world.

RISHONIM: lit. the first ones; European scholars of the eleventh through the 15th century.

ROSH CHODESH: the first day of a new month.

RO'EH BASHOSHANIM: a depiction of God as a Shepherd carrying roses instead of a staff.

ROSH KOLLEL: a rabbi in charge of a *kollel*.

ROSH MESIVTA: a principal of a yeshivah.

ROSH YESHIVAH: a rabbi who heads a yeshivah.

SEFER, SEFARIM: book(s).

SEFER/SIFREI TORAH: Torah scroll(s).

SEMICHAH: Rabbinical ordination.

SEUDAH SHELISHIT/S: the third Sabbath meal.

SHALIACH: lit. a messenger; an agent.

SHALOM BAYIS: lit. peace at home; marital harmony.

SHALOM ZACHAR: lit. welcoming a boy; a open-house spread set up on the Fri. night before a baby boy's *bris*.

SHANAH ALEF, SHANAH BET, SHANAH GIMMEL: first year, second year, third year.

SHAS: the six orders of the *Mishnah*; the Talmud.

SHE'EILAH, SHE'EILOS: halachic question(s) referred to a rav.

SHEHECHEYANU: the blessing recited before fulfilling certain mitzvos for the first time that season.

SHEMIRAH: protection.

SHIDDUCH: a matrimonial match.

SHIUR, SHIURIM: Torah lecture(s).

SHMUESSIN: mussar (ethics) discourses.

SHULCHAN ARUCH: the authoritative Code of Jewish law, written by Rabbi Yoseph Karo in the 16th century.

SIMCHAS TORAH: lit. Joy of Torah; the holiday of rejoicing with the Torah celebrated at the end of Sukkos.

SIMCHAT BEIT HASHO'EIVAH: lit. rejoicing at the house of the water drawing; a celebration during Sukkos in the Holy Temple, still celebrated with music and dancing every night of Chol Hamoed Sukkos.

SIYATTA DISHMAYA: Heavenly assistance.

SIMCHAH, SMACHOT/S: lit. happy time(s); special occasion(s).

SUGYAS, SUGYA: topics, topic.

SUKKAH: lit. a booth; the Torah commands living in booths for the seven days of the holiday of Tabernacles (Sukkos).

TALMID CHACHAM: a Torah scholar.

TALMID/TALMIDIM: student(s).

TANACH: the entire Bible.

TISHAH B'AV: lit. the ninth day of the month of Av when the Temple was destroyed which is the Jewish Nation's greatest day of mourning.

TZADDIK, TZADDIKIM: a righteous man/men.

TZADDIK GAMUR: a completely righteous man.

TZADEIKES: a righteous woman.

TZEITCHEM L'SHALOM: lit; may you leave in peace; farewell.

TZIDKUS: righteousness.

YAAKOV AVINU: Jacob our patriarch.

YAMIM TOVIM: Holidays.

YARCHEI KALLAH: a yearly assemblage of Torah learning.

YIZKOR: the prayer said on the three festivals in memory of deceased relatives.

YOM TOV: a holiday.

YETZER HARA: the evil inclination.

YEREI SHAMAYIM: a person or people who have fear of Heaven.

ZECHUS: merit.

ZEMANEI HAYOM: halachic times.

ZEVACHIM (GEMARA): a tractate of *Gemara*.

ZT"L: the acronym for *zecher tzaddik livrachah* — may a righteous person's memory be a blessing.